Crystal Path

Based on a true story

Ann Eva Graves

Ann Eva Graves

During the early fifties, my parents suffered
tragedies that changed their lives forever.
The hardships my patents went through
inspired me to write this book. May we be
together again when life is over.

Crystal Path

Copyright © 2009 by Ann Eva Graves

Printed in the United States of America

ISBN: 978-0-615-28972-4

Dedication

This book is dedicated to my parents. My father's name was Reverend Lawrence N. Sumner, an old-fashioned country preacher in the hills of East Tennessee. Dad accepted the Lord while working in a coal mine. He was Born: February 7, 1910 and Died: December 26, 1962.

My mother's name was Rosa Lee Adkins (Sumner). She was Born: February 24, 1920 and Died: December 30, 1996. After my dad's death, she worked very hard raising the four youngest children. My mother died at the age of seventy-six of Amyotrophic Lateral Sclerosis (Lou Gehrig's disease). I am thankful that I was blessed with such caring and loving parents.

Dad and Mom, 1959   Mom 1936

Contents

~~ Chapter One ~~

The year was 1953, in the small town of Coalfield, with a population of about 500. Although I was three and four years old at the time, I remember my dad telling wonderful stories about his dogs and their hunting trips together.

During the early 1950s in East Tennessee, hunting wild game was a way of life for families trying to survive the hard times. People were poor and couldn't afford to buy meat at the grocery store. They hunted deer, wild turkey, wild hog, rabbit, squirrel and occasionally, raccoon. It was a convenient way to provide for a large family.

Reverend John Winters and his family lived in a small five-room house on Ridge Hill Road, a gravel road about three miles from Highway 62. Most of the people in the community and surrounding areas knew Reverend Winters. He had preached throughout Morgan County and in several surrounding counties. He was the pastor of a small country church at Mosey Grove.

The church had white wooden siding, three wood-framed windows on each side, and a small steeple on top. Inside were 12 wooden benches. In front was a pulpit, and in front of the pulpit was a wooden altar for praying. In the corner was a piano.

It was a spiritual church-house of worship, where people went to obtain nourishment for their souls, a country church with simple folks who made everyone who entered feel welcome. The presence of God was felt throughout.

When Sister Minnie Smith raised her hands to praise the Lord, people felt warmness in their hearts. Each time Brother Ed Jones stood to testify, they felt love and kindness in his voice. These were God-fearing Christians who had compassion and love for everyone.

John was a handsome man of medium build, 6' tall, and 210 lbs., with black hair and brown eyes. His features showed Cherokee Indian in his ancestry. He was a kind Christian man who would help anyone in need. He was also an extremely amiable and compassionate man, and was a good judge of character.

However, sometimes he showed a firm hand with his children. But his heart was filled with kindness. His wife, Rosie, was a medium-built woman with a round face and kind eyes. She was an easy-going person, who always seemed happy. She stood 5' 5", and had dark brown hair and brown eyes. She was an extremely virtuous woman, with a good heart, deep faith and giving spirit.

The Winters family home was originally on Windridge Mountain east of Mosey Grove. Reverend John Winters worked for Morgan County grading gravel roads. Most county roads were graded every six to eight weeks. Several families lived on the mountain, and the roads were extremely rough and rocky. The other employees who worked for the county wouldn't even attempt to clear the roads across the mountain. They were narrow and steep in many places, and had no guard rails.

Nevertheless, John spoke to his boss, Mr. Clarence Duncan, about making it possible for the school bus to take the children to school.

He entered the office and found his boss had been talking with another employee, Jerry Dodson. As he walked in, Jerry was leaving.

"Yessir, Mister Duncan, I'll start on that job right away. Mornin' John," Jerry said, as he walked toward the door.

"Hello, Jerry. The boss gotcha busy already this mornin'?" John asked as he ran his fingers through his hair.

"Yep, he's tougher'n a one-eared alley cat; ye better watch 'im." Jerry laughed, as he spoke.

John approached his boss, and Mr. Duncan motioned for him to sit down near his desk. John sat down and cleared his throat. "Mister Duncan, I'd like to talk to ya 'bout somethin' this mornin'."

"Okay, John, whatcha wanna talk about?"

"Well, sir, I been thinkin' 'bout clearin' the roads cross the Windridge Mountin in Coalfield, so the school bus can pick up all the childrun who live up thar. The young-uns have to walk several miles to catch the bus, and many cain't even go to school durin' the snowy winter. Well, anyhow, I thought I'd talk to ya about it, an' find out if would be all right."

Mr. Duncan rubbed his chin, leaned back in his chair, thought for a moment and shook his head. "Well, John, yer a better man than I am. Some places up thar are hard for a horse to get thru much less a road grader." He smiled and continued, "I'm real impressed. If yer willin' to give it a try, then I'll give ya tha go-ahead. I got to tell ya, nobody else would even attempt such a job. When ya wanna start on it?"

"Right away. I was aimin' to start first thing tomorrah mornin'."

"Well, ya got the job. An' take as long as you need. If ya get all the roads, or should I say, horse trails, cleared across the mountin, I'll be amazed," Mr. Duncan said.

Early the next morning, John climbed on his road grader and began slowly making his way up the mountain. He had to grade over the road several times.

Frequently, he had to dig out boulders and move them aside. Some places were especially narrow and hard to get through, which caused him to break two grader blades.

The people on the mountain were overjoyed to see him fixing the roads. They offered him drinking water and lunch. For some folks living on the mountain, this was the first time they had seen such a big machine on their roads. Without repair of the roads, people had to walk or ride a horse down the mountain just to get to Brooks Grocery Store, the only store in the community.

They loved John for making a way for their children to go to school, and they looked up to him as their hero in hard times.

The third day on the job, just off another road, John noticed a *"For Sale"* sign at the end of a driveway. The house was on a small hill and looked fairly new, with white siding. He stopped his road grader, climbed down and walked up the bumpy driveway. A yellow cat ran behind the house and a rooster crowed.

As John stood outside the front door, he looked around and thought the size was just what his family needed. He knocked on the door. A few seconds later, a small woman came to the door. She was 5' 2" and in her late fifties, with gray running through her dark auburn hair. "Kin I help ya?" she asked, as she wiped her hands on her apron.

"Yes, ma'am. My name's John Winters, an' I was gradin' the roads today, an' noticed yer sign at the end of the driveway."

"Yessir, I'm sellin' the house on accounta I'm movin'. Oh, whar's my manners? Name's Sally Wilson. As I was sayin', I'm a-sellin' the house. Ya see, my husband, *God rest his soul*, started buildin' the house 'bout a year ago." She paused and looked off, then continued, "He passed away three months ago, an' I don't wanna live up heah on this mountin all by my ownself. Besides, ain't easy livin' here without my husband an' all my recollections in this house. I gotta daughter who lives in Knoxv'lle, an' that's whar I figah on movin'," she explained as she opened the door wider.

"How much are ya askin' for the house, Missus Wilson?"

She hesitated for a moment while she adjusted her apron. "The house hain't finished on the inside, and some walls hain't finished neither. If'n ya want tha house the way tis, ya kin have it fer a thousand dollars, an' five acres comes with the house."

Curious about his character, she studied his features, and found kindness in his eyes. "I got some hens out back I'll leave heah. And upstairs in the loft is some jars o' green beans 'n' pickles I canned last fall. Yer kinfolk is more'n welcome to eat 'em if ya de-cide to buy my house."

"Yes, ma'am, I shore am interested. You see I live in Sunbright now. I'm the pastor here at the church at Mosey Grove, an' I'd like to find a house closer to church."

"Well, go on ahead an' look around a bit," she said, motioning with her hand. "I'm busy in tha kitchen."

"Thankee, Missus Wilson. I'll mosey around back 'n' have a look-around."

John noticed that an acre had been cleared for a large garden, and that the house had good shade trees on the south side. He could see the water well behind the house just outside the back door, two large apple trees and a hen house with about 20 hens and a rooster, surrounded by a fence. He was behind the house looking at the water well when Mrs. Wilson came to the back door with a tall glass of water. "Revrun Winters, would ya like a cup o' water?"

He wiped the perspiration from his brow. "I shore would 'preciate it," he answered as she handed the glass to him. "Looks like it's gonna to be another hot day," John commented.

"Yessir. If'n it's like yesterdy, it's gonna be a scorcher. That well shore has good water, crystal clear. Down yonder path in the woods is an open field, an' just beyond is a coal mine. I use the coal fer heatin' durin' the winter. Part of the coal mine is on this heah land, an' they lemme get coal fer free, but I got ta tote it back to the house by my own self.

Shading his eyes, John looked up, "I do wanna buy the house, Missus Wilson. I'll try 'n' get the money in a few days. I'll bring my wife with me, so she can look at the place. If she likes it, we'll buy it. I better get back to work. An' thankee for the water," he said as he handed her the empty cup.

~~~~~

The Winters family moved into the house in April of 1953. The first task John accomplished was building an altar in the woods 80 yards behind the house. He gathered round flat stones shaped in such a way that they would fit together perfectly, providing a place to kneel and pray. John believed the only way to have joy in your soul and stay in fellowship with the Lord is to study the Bible daily and have a prayer life. This was a subject he often preached.

The family worked hard to finish repairing the inside of the house themselves by putting up two walls in one room to create three rooms. To the right of the living room, or "sitting room," as it was called, was a door leading into a larger room, which made three bedrooms. The first one, just off the sitting room, was John and Rosie's bedroom. From that bedroom was a second room, and, in back, a third room.

They couldn't afford to buy wood or paneling for the walls to separate each room, so Rosie collected new stove and refrigerator cardboard boxes from the store. She measured the pieces of cardboard, cut them to size and nailed each piece to the walls.

Rosie was more skilled at carpentry than her husband. John was all thumbs and had a hard time with a hammer and nails. Rosie, on the other hand, could take a handsaw and hammer and fix just about anything.

The house had wood-framed windows. They put vinyl rugs in the kitchen and sitting room. The bedroom floors were wood. A wall separated the sitting room from the kitchen. Stairs led from the kitchen to a large loft, where Rosie stored her canned goods.

Outside the back door, four steps led to the well. Two vertical poles seven feet high on either side were attached to a pole across the top. A pulley over the well attached to the horizontal pole in the middle. A rope ran through the pulley, and one end was tied to a long bucket for bringing up water. At the top was a ring. When pulled upward, it opened a valve at the bottom to release the water.

A cast-iron stove was in the sitting room for heating during the winter months. They had to carry coal from the coal mine to the house in a large brown sack, called a poke. The house had no hot water heater or bathroom. A privy was located 40 yards behind the house. Rosie built a pot chair, so that the children wouldn't have to go outside and use the privy at night and during winter months.

In the process of building it, she cut a hole in the middle of a straight-back wooden chair and placed a pot in the middle, with a lid to cover the pot. The hole was somewhat smaller than the pot rim so it would fit into the hole, but not fall through. She decorated the pot chair by making a pretty cushion to cover the seat, and she placed a ruffled skirt, to match the cushion, around the bottom. Rosie used flour sacks for material.

John bought the flour in 25-pound sacks for 20 cents each, which was more economical for a large family. When the sack was empty, Rosie unraveled and washed it, and she made flour sack panties, pillowcases and dresses. The sack came stitched on one side, therefore, when unraveled, it was one large piece of fabric. Most of the fabric had decorative designs and flower prints.

To wash dishes, they heated water on the stove in two large dish pans, one to wash and the other to rinse. Afterward, the water was then thrown outdoors.

Each week, they had to draw 12 to 14 buckets of water from the well to do laundry. They had an agitator washing machine that had two ringers, one tightly on top of the other, which turned in opposite directions. The ringers, attached to the side, would swing to the middle when in use. Rosie placed each piece of clothing through the double ringers, one at a time.

She placed the clothes in a second tub to rinse them, and ran each piece through the ringer to get out the excess water before hanging them on a clothesline, which she created by tying a rope between two trees. To keep the line from sagging in the middle, she made a prop from the branch of a small tree, which was forked on one end. When the clothes were dry, it was time to do the week's ironing. Rosie used a large vinegar bottle with a tight-fitting lid as a sprinkling device. She punched several holes in the lid with a small nail so that when the bottle was shaken upside-down, the water sprinkled the clothing.

With little money to buy food, John planted a large garden every year. They grew most of their food except grain and cornmeal. During winter, he hunted deer, squirrel and rabbit. They had fresh eggs, and they were grateful to Mrs. Wilson for giving them the hens.

Rosie always baked a large hen for Thanksgiving, with cornbread stuffing and all the fixings. Each year, Rosie canned green beans, tomatoes, peas, squash, sauerkraut, okra and corn. She made apple jelly from the apple trees in the backyard, and grape jelly from their vines.

To keep the potatoes from freezing through the winter months, John dug a large hole in the ground three feet deep and covered it with a sheet of tin. The family worked extremely hard, but they were strong and accustomed to working as they did.

~~ Chapter Two ~~

The Jones family lived up the road an eighth of a mile from the Winters, and the two families became good friends. They, too, were very poor, and lived in a four room house with rough wood for siding. The house was dark brown with a large porch across the front.

Their driveway was especially rough and rocky. Clifford Jones and his wife Daisy had four children. Clifford was of medium build, with a touch of red in his light brown hair. He appeared to be of Irish descent. Daisy was a slender woman with long light brown hair and hazel eyes.

Their youngest, Carrie, was four years old. Nicknamed "Kooter," she was the prettiest child, with big blue eyes and long curly blonde hair. She was shy and quiet. Jake, seven, was a mysterious little boy with light-brown hair and blue eyes. The third child, Faye, was ten, and also had big blue eyes and blonde, curly hair. Faye was a happy and loving child. Brenda, the eldest, at 13, had large hazel eyes and long light-brown hair, much like her mother's. She was of great help to her mother, protective of her younger siblings, and she seemed much older and more mature than her age.

Two days after the Winters family moved into the house, Clifford Jones drove over to welcome them to the neighborhood. He wanted to thank John for clearing the roads across the mountain. His family was most grateful that their children had a way to get to school during the winter months. They knew John was a kind Christian man, but he also became their hero.

As Clifford came up the driveway, he saw John working on the motor of his panel truck, and he stopped just behind him. John moved his head from beneath the hood and wiped his hands on a rag he had placed in his back pocket. Clifford extended out his hand in a friendly gesture, and John did likewise.

"Name's Clifford Jones; ah live up the road apiece. You might could say it's jes a hop an' a skip over ta my place. Anyhow, ah jes wanna ta give ya a friendly welcome," he said with a big smile.

"I'm John Winters. We just moved in a couple 'o' days ago." He returned the smile.

"Ah done heered aboutcha clearin' tha roads cross tha mountin. Ah shore do thankee, Mister Winters, fer doin' that so's our young-uns kin git to school. Fer all yer hard work, ah thought I'd come on over heah, 'n' be neighborly an' see if ya might need me to plow that thar field next to yer house so's ya kin plant yer garden," Clifford offered. "Yer gonna plant a garden, ain'tcha?"

"Ya don't have to do that, Clifford. I ain't got any money to pay ye right now."

"Why! I'd be glad to, ah always got a garden ever year. Don'tcha even think 'bout payin' me. Yer my neighbor; ah like helpin' my neighbor ever now 'n' agin. I'll bring my mule over here to yer place an' start on it in a few days. Bertha, that ol' mule o' mine's the bes' worker ah ever did see. She'll git yer field plowed lick-a-de-split."

"I'm much obliged, Clifford, it shore is nice to have good neighbors. If ever you need help, just lemme know."

The following day, Clifford brought his mule over and began to plow the field. John wanted to plant enough vegetables so they would have plenty of food to last through the winter. The children would help tend to the garden by hoeing each week to keep it free of weeds.

When the plowing was completed, Clifford tied a large log behind the mule and let her pull it over the ground to break up clumps and make it level. John recognized Clifford as a caring person, and was proud to have him for a neighbor.

The next morning, John drove down the mountain to Brook's Grocery. It was the only store in Coalfield. He parked his truck in front of the store and saw Ed Jones sitting on a bench in front. Mr. Jones, also known as *"Brother Ed,"* attended Mosey Grove Church.

He was a kind old man in his late 70s. On his head was a black small-rim hat and a pipe always extended from the corner of his mouth, but he never inhaled the smoke. The pipe gave him comfort and provided something to keep him occupied.

Ed sat quietly on the bench watching John as he parked his truck. He liked to sit in front of the store and talk to everyone who entered. When anyone was in need, he was willing to lend a helping hand. He was thought of as a guardian angel in the community. John had a special friendship with Ed and his family. When he saw John walking toward the store entry, he extended his hand in a friendly handshake, "Howdee, Revrun Winters. Yer kinfolk been gettin' along all right?"

"Doin' just fine, Brother Ed. We been missin' ya at church."

"Sorry, ah hain't been ta service these past two Sundys, but ah been a-feelin' kinda poorly. This ol' body's startin' ta slow down, Revrun. Oh, but I'm ready ta go when the Good Lord calls me on home."

John returned the handshake. "We been prayin' that ya'd get to feelin' better, Brother Ed. We miss seein' ya in yer spot on the front bench."

"Thankee, Revrun. I'll come to church when ah commence ta feelin' a bit better," he said, and he moved the pipe to the other side of his mouth.

It didn't take long for John to finish his shopping. As he walked out of the store, Ed motioned for him to stop. He had been waiting patiently for John to return.

"Hey, Revrun Winters, how'd ya like two good huntin' dawgs? Their mama died last week. 'Em pups are only about two months old. They jes' been weaned. My Bessie had eight pups, an' two 'em died when they was borned. My nephew, Tom, took two of 'em. Said he was a-fixin' ta train 'em fer fox huntin'. An' ah give two away yesterday." A sad look crossed his face. "My Bessie come upon an ol' black bahr up on Pine Ridge last week 'n' nary made it back home. That ol' bahr done tored her all ta pieces. He musta swung at 'er with his paw an' hit 'er head, on accounta her neck was broke. My nephew found 'er the next day after she come up missin'. He done buried her behind tha house near the wood line. Lemme tell ya, when she was young, she coulda whupped that ol' bahr." He smiled at the memory. "She was the bes' huntin' dawg ah ever had, an' right smart, she were. She could hunt anythin' she fixed on." He shook his head slowly, "Yessir, ah had Bessie fer bout 13 yar, an' I'm a-gonna miss her real bad. Lemme tell ya, me 'n' ol' Bessie had some good huntin' times together. I'm too old ta go huntin' now. Ah need ta find 'em pups a good home, somebody who'll hunt with 'em an' make 'em happy."

"I shore do like fox-huntin', Brother Ed. I been thinkin' 'bout findin' me another dawg. Maybe the pups'll make some good huntin' dawgs."

"Ifn they're anythin' like ol' Bessie, you'll have some fine foxhounds," he said proudly. "These two pups are the bes' in the litter, an' ah been savin' 'em till after they was weaned, so ah might could give 'em to ya, Revrun, on accounta yer a good frien' an' 'em pups are special ta me."

John, appeared pleased, "Shore, I'm always glad to get good huntin' dawgs. An' I consider you a good frien', too, Brother Ed. I'll come by your place tomorrah 'n' pick 'em up."

"Okay, I'll have 'em ready fer ya."

~~~~~~

The next evening, John drove his old Dodge panel truck down to Mr. Jones' house. As he pulled into the driveway, there was Ed with his pipe hanging from his mouth, and a small brimmed hat on his head, sitting on his front porch whittling with a pocketknife he'd had for years. Ed motioned with his hand, and called from the front porch, as John got out of his truck.

"C'mon in, Revrun Winters. 'Em pups are ready. Are ye hungry? Supper's jes about set. I'll git Dottie ta set an extry plate on the table. Ya can sit ah spell cain't ya?"

"Much obliged, Brother Ed, but Rosie'll be expectin' me home for supper di-reckly, so's I cain't stay long. I better be a-gettin' the pups 'n' head back home."

"Well, let's go fetch 'em then. They're jes' around back," he tried to stand up. The arthritis in his back caused him difficulty. "Ah already named 'em, but if ya wanna change 'em, that's fine."

Ed walked slowly, as he led John to the back of the house. As he got closer to the pups, he extended a finger out and pointed. "Now this'n heah was borned first, so's ah named 'im Speed. The other'n ah named Fred, after my dawg ah had when ah was jes' a boy about ten yar old. I won't nary fergit that ol' fella." he laughed. "Lemme tell ya, ol' Fred 'n' me use ta romp round in tha woods near our home place all day long. He'd follered me everwhar I went. Ah guess he was more a pet than a huntin' dawg. Ah reckon ever' boy needs a good dawg."

"That's right, Brother Ed, ever' boy needs a four-footed best friend," John answered back, with a grin.

"Ah looked 'em over real good after they was borned, an' ah knew right away these two pups was gonna make some fine huntin' dawgs. Ah kin tell by the shapes o' their paws."

"Ya can tell by their paws?"

"Yup. Lemme show ya sump'n." He bent down and reached for Fred, holding him gently in his hand. Holding his front paw between his fingers, he said, "See this dewclaw heah on the side o' his paw? Ifn a dawg's got dewclaws, an' these two pups shore got 'em, then ya knowed that's a smart dawg." He squinted, and shook his head, "Why, ah wouldn't have a dawg, lessen he got dewclaws!"

"I never paid much attention to that, Brother Ed." he said with a smile.

"My Bessie had dewclaws, an' she was a right smart huntin' dawg," he remarked, as he bent down and gently placed Fred back on the ground.

"I'm glad ya told me how to pick out a smart dawg, Brother Ed. And thankee for givin' me the best pups in the litter."

"They's special dawgs to me, Revrun." He glanced away, trying not to show emotion. "Ah jes wished ah was a young fella agin, so's ah might could train em, an' go huntin' sometime. That's one thing ah miss, goin' huntin' with ol' Bessie. When ah was young, me 'n' 'er usta hunt all over these heah woods. Ol' Bessie was such a smart dawg, an' she could hunt anything she set 'er mind to." He paused, looked at John, and smiled. "But ah reckon we all got ta grow old, an' pass on some time er another," he added, as he placed his thumbs behind his overall straps.

"I'm shore I'll enjoy huntin' with 'em, Brother Ed. They're gonna make some fine huntin' dawgs, I'll bet." He walked to the truck and called back to Ed, "If thar's anythin' I can do for ya, just holler," he said, and placed the pups in his truck.

After bringing the pups home that evening, John made a bed for them near the back door. He was growing fond of them already, and he had a good feeling Brother Ed was right, *they were going to be some fine hunting dogs,* and he was eager to begin their training.

Being tired, John went to bed early. Before retiring for the night, he peeked out the back door to check on his dogs and found them curled up close together on their bed, fast asleep. After his head hit the pillow, it didn't take long for John to fall asleep and he dreamed:

He was sitting on the back steps behind his house. The dogs were jumping up on his leg, wanting him to pet them. They seemed so small. Speed tried to push Fred aside so he could get all the attention. They were very strong pups and extremely playful. What a team they were!

Then he was training the pups. They were two months old, and he was teaching them to fox hunt. Using the drag technique with a foxtail, he pulled it on the ground in the woods near the house. The pups were following his commands especially well, and they seemed eager to please their master. They followed him everywhere he went. It was as if he had two extra shadows besides his own.

Then they got older, and he began to take them deeper into the woods. They were always together, and John noticed they were learning hunting skills from each other. They were born with great hunting instincts and an eagerness to learn. The pups began to run. He found them cute, with their long legs moving fast and their ears flapping in the wind. Suddenly, they began to run with great force, as though they were racing. He had never seen them run so fast.

As he watched, they changed, from pups to fullgrown dogs, and they continued to race against the wind. They were using every muscle as they ran faster and faster. He had never seen them with so much strength. All at once, they reached the edge of a high cliff. Quickly, they stopped and looked over the edge. All they could see was total darkness.

John found himself standing opposite his dogs on another high cliff, at least 50 yards from where the dogs were. A great gulf was between them. A great gulf of darkness. He thought how terrible it would be to fall into the abyss. Into total nothingness. Just darkness forever.

A troubled frown creased his brow. He glanced around. There was nowhere to go. How would he get off the cliff? More than that, how would he get his dogs back? It was a box canyon, with no way to reach the dogs and no way for the dogs to come to him. The situation looked hopeless. If they jumped, they would die.

They started to bark, wanting desperately to come to him. He felt deep despair. It seemed he had lost his dogs forever. His heart ached as he looked over at them barking and pleading for help. Speed barked in an urgent tone, as though he were trying to speak, while Fred made a pitiful crying sound.

A deep yearning consumed John's whole body. He knew that without a miracle the dogs would be lost forever. He began to pray: "Please Lord, make a way for me to get my dawgs back."

A soft iridescent light began to shine on the dogs. John could see all the colors of the rainbow. The light got brighter and started to twirl, reflecting colors around the dogs. Slowly, the light began to form a crystal-clear narrow path. The pathway gleamed and sparkled from the light.

Gradually, the light began to push a pathway from the edge of the cliff, where the dogs stood, toward the cliff where John stood. He stared in amazement, as the iridescent light twirled and pushed the crystal path inch-by-inch, until it reached the edge where he was. It was three feet wide, appeared suspended in mid-air, connected to the cliff at his feet; and it went across to the other side, where the dogs were.

When John raised his head and looked back over the great canyon, he saw Brother Ed standing beside the dogs. A soft glow surrounded Brother Ed's body, and he was trying to encourage the dogs to cross.

John called to them loudly, "C'mon, Fred, it's okay. C'mon over, Speed. You can make it." Speed stepped on the crystal path first, and when he realized he was safe and wouldn't fall, he continued, walking slowly toward John. Fred hesitated, stood still, and watched Speed as he made his way across.

John called, "C'mon over, Fred. It's okay, you can make it, boy." Fred remained still and whined. He desperately wanted to go to John, but something seemed to hold him back.

At last, Speed reached John and happily greeted his master. He noticed Fred was not behind him and was still on the other side. Speed barked at Fred, trying to communicate that it was safe to walk on the path, but Fred just barked and whimpered, as though scared. Speed carefully stepped on the crystal path again and slowly made his way to Fred. After reaching the other side, he greeted Fred with urgent whining sounds. When he turned to step back onto the path, Fred eagerly followed.

John called to them, "C'mon back, you can make it. C'mon Speed, bring yer brother over to me. Ata- boy, keep a-goin'. Yer almost here." As they came closer, John smiled. He eagerly watched his dogs make their way to him across the crystal path. When they reached the end, they jumped onto John's chest to greet him. John's cup overflowed with joy and happiness.

While greeting the dogs, he looked back at Brother Ed, and the soft light surrounding his body continued to glow. John waved at him, and motioned with his hand for him to walk across the crystal path and join them. However, Brother Ed stood motionless, not saying a word, looking at them with a joyous and peaceful expression. Somehow, John knew Brother Ed would have to remain on the other side. He realized there must be a special reason Brother Ed couldn't join them.

He glanced down and found the light was pulling the crystal path back to the other side where Brother Ed stood. After the crystal path receded, the light became brighter and slowly started to twirl again. As the soft iridescent light reflected rainbow colors around Brother Ed, he slowly rose into the light and disappeared. John felt peacefulness as he watched Brother Ed became one with the light.

Slowly, the cliffs moved toward each other, joined, and made the darkness disappear.

John wakened and realized he was in bed. The dream seemed real. He could still feel the dogs' paws on his chest and feel the warm glow from the rainbow light that had shined upon them. He wondered why Brother Ed was in his dream, and he thought, *What a strange dream. It was unusual to see my dawgs fully grown.*

~~ Chapter Three ~~

At the breakfast table the next morning, John told his family about his dream. "I had a dream last night about my pups an' Brother Ed. For some reason, they were no bigger'n tater bugs an' a-runnin faster than greased lightnin', I never seen pups run so fast. All a suddenlike, they was full-grown dawgs. 'Twas queer to see 'em grown. And then, a be-utiful light was ah shinin' on 'em. It twirled with different rainbow colors. The light was so amazin', an' pure, an' it gimme such a peaceful an' happy feelin'. It'd be nice to feel that-a-way all the time. It seemed so real."

"Is thar more, John?" Rosie asked.

"Shore. Brother Ed was a-standin' on another cliff with my dawgs, a far piece away, with the purtiest glow around him. Just a-lookin at it was amazin'. It was as if he suddenly appeared on the other cliff to help my dawgs walk on the crystal path over to me. After the dawgs made their way across, the colored lights got to twirlin' around Brother Ed. And then he started to rise up real slow 'n' faded into the light. Then I woke up. It seemed so real. I gotta tell Brother Ed about my dream the next time I see 'im." John paused. "But, it was only a dream," he said, as he took another sip of his coffee.

"Daddy, it sounds just like a miracle!" Becky said, wide-eyed.

"Or like a fairy tale," Laura said.

"Daddy, tell us more stories," Neva pleaded. "I like to hear ya tell stories."

"It ain't no story, it's a dream," Lula added.

"Yeah, an' dreams cain't come true," Shane said.

"Yeah, they do. Sometimes dreams do come true, don't they Daddy?" Ellie asked.

"Well, in a way yer both right. A dream is just a dream, but sometimes amazin' things happen we cain't explain. I suppose it's like a miracle. Some men in the Bible had dreams from God, either to warn 'em about sump'n or to receive some kinda message. Just like the dream Joseph had, to warn 'im to flee with Mary 'n' Jesus. Sometimes our dreams do have some kinda meanin'," he tried to explain.

After breakfast, Rosie asked John to go to Brooks Grocery Store to pick up flour and cornmeal. She had so much work to do; she didn't have time to go. Rosie didn't know how to drive.

As he drove down the mountain toward Brooks Grocery, John's thoughts were about his dream and the special glow from the soft iridescent light. He was thinking about Brother Ed and the way he disappeared into the light. He asked himself aloud, *"Why did I have such a queer dream an' see my dawgs fully grown? Was there a special meanin' to the dream?"*

He was in deep thought, and suddenly realized he had reached his destination. He parked his truck in front of the store and went in. After gathering his groceries, he set them on the counter.

"Didja hear about Ed Jones?"

"Naw, I ain't heard a thing about Brother Ed. What happen?"

"Word is he done passed away last night." Mr. Brooks said.

John raised his brow, in surprise.

"His neighbor, Ruth Jenkins, come into the store this mornin'. She just left a few minutes ago. She said Dottie got up early this mornin' to start breakfus, an' when she tried to wake 'im, she found out he done passed away in bed. It scared her so bad she got ta screamin an' woke up their boy, Isaiah. Ruth said it took a long time fer the boy to calm 'er down. He told Ruth his dad had such a peaceful look on his face. An' a smile."

"I hate to hear about Brother Ed passin'. I'm shore lotsa folks'll miss 'im. I shore will." John was still thinking about the dream, and he wondered if the dream showed him Brother Ed's passing away. And what about the dawgs? He couldn't put the meaning together. He didn't say anything to Mr. Brooks about it.

"I'll forever be beholdin' to Brother Ed," John said. "He gimme two pups just yesterdy. I'm fixin' to start trainin 'em to fox hunt. They seem to be real smart an' playful too." He paused. "Yessir, I'll surely miss 'im. He was a kind soul, and always in good spirit."

"Yup, Ed was a kind man. He'd help anybody, an' give 'em the shirt off his back," Mr. Brooks added.

"He shore would. Ya know, Mr. Brooks, someday the Lord's gonna have a gatherin' we cain't imagine. We'll see all our friends 'n' loved ones who've gone on before us with a grand homecomin' that'll last throughout eternity. An' what a special day that'll be! I got to find out when they're havin' his funeral, so I can pay my last respects," John said sadly.

"I don't know, Revrun, but Ruth heard he wanted you to do the preachin' at his service."

"I'll stop by an' talk to Dottie, an' if that's what he wanted, I'd be right honored." He picked up his supplies, got into his truck and drove home.

Three days later, John preached at Brother Ed's funeral and paid his last respects to his good friend. The church overflowed with flowers. With so many friends and loved ones, the church was completely filled, with some folks standing outside.

Dottie sat on the front bench with their son, daughter and son-in-law. Behind them were other family members and grandchildren and great-grandchildren. Brother Ed had requested two songs for his service. As the singers finished the first song, *'Where We'll Never Grow Old'*.

John walked to the pulpit, and cleared his throat. He looked at the gathering, and spoke in a soft tone. "We come together today to honor an' pay our last respects to a family member an' great friend, Brother Edward Isaiah Jones. He was 79 years old when the Lord called 'im on home last Sundy night. He was a beloved member of Mosey Grove Church. Many folks in this community an' surroundin' areas will miss Mr. Jones tremendously. He worked most o' his life in the coal mines, an' then owned a sawmill compny in Coalfield, 'til he retard at 63. As a matter a fact, Brother Ed was a-workin' with me in the coal mines when I accepted the Lord into my life. Brother Ed usta talk to me about the Lord from time to time while we were aworkin'." He cleared his throat, trying to hold back emotion. "It seemed he was always tryin' to help others."

John glanced around the room before continuing. "He is survived by his be-utiful wife, Dottie, of 55 years; their son, Isaiah Jones; daughter and son inlaw, Emily and William Hart, who live in Coalfield; and several other famly members. They were blessed with twelve grandchildrun, eight great-grandchildrun, an' two great-great-grandchildrun.

Those who went to be with the Lord before 'im was Brother Ed's folks; his two sons, Zachary of Oak Ridge, an Lawrence of Deer Lodge; brother Theodore of Coalfield; an sister Mae Stokes of Oak Dale. All his family 'n' friens in Coalfield an' surroundin' communities will recollect Mr. Jones as a kind an' givin' man, for it seemed he touched all our hearts at some point in our lives."

John opened his Bible and began, "If ya'd like to foller along, I'd like to start readin' from 1 Thessalonians, Chapter 4, verses 13 to 18:

But I would not have you to be ignorant, brethren, concerning them which are asleep, that ye sorrow not, even as others, which have no hope.

For if we believe that Jesus died and rose again, even so them also which sleep in Jesus will God bring with him.

For this we say unto you by the word of the Lord, that we which are alive [and] remain unto the coming of the Lord shall not prevent them which are asleep.

For the Lord himself shall descend from heaven with a shout, with the voice of the archangel, and with the trump of God: and the dead in Christ shall rise first:

Then we which are alive [and] remain shall be caught up together with them in the clouds, to meet the Lord in the air: and so shall we ever be with the Lord.

Wherefore comfort one another with these words.

He glanced up, and continued, "The first time Jesus came down an' walked on earth, he was as a humble child, with love an' compassion. He willfully laid down his life an' died for our sins. However, the next time He returns, He will return with great Glory! Those that have their sins covered by the blood of Jesus, that have accepted Him as their personal Savior, will rise to meet Him in the air, to be with Him forever more." As he spoke, he felt the love of God flowing deep in his soul.

The church was quiet. All eyes were fixed on Reverend Winters. "The Bible tells us to comfort one another with these words. For one day soon, we'll all be together again with all our friens 'n' loved ones who've gone on before us. Brother Ed has gone on home to be with the Lord, 'twas his time to leave this walk o' life, to face his eternity. He's now in a peaceful place, waitin' for the Lord to return an' bring 'im on home. Yes, it is comfortin' to believe that one day we will all be together again. God has promised in his Word of that blessed day we can all look forward to." Energized by the Glory of God, he continued, "Brother Jones was a fine example of what brotherly love ought to be. We'll not ferget him, for he was a great blessin' to each of us. May the Lord bless his family, an' keep 'em in the shelter of His arms, 'till His return. Now, if the singers would begin singin'."

John retreated to the bench behind him. At Brother Ed's request, through his wife, the singers began to softly sing, *'Amazing Grace'*. Before the song was finished, not a dry eye existed in the church.

~~ Chapter Four ~~

Three days had passed since the funeral. John continued to grade the roads across the mountain, and he often thought about Ed Jones. He had seemed like a second father to John, and he missed him deeply.

The sun had just peeked over the mountain, and John drove his machine slowly through a narrow area in a road, trying to push away some dirt from a steep embankment to widen the road, when he noticed a dark green house and a woman running toward the road with a child in her arms. The child appeared to be about two years old. He guessed the woman to be in her early thirties. She was slender, with light brown hair. She cried and screamed in panic, "Help! Help! Oh, please help!"

John immediately stopped his road grader and got off. The woman continued to run toward the road as he rushed toward her. She had a terrified expression.

"My li'l girl drank some Clorox! Oh, help 'er, please help 'er!"

John spoke in a soft tone, as he tried to calm the woman. "Let's take 'er up to the house. How much Clorox did she drank?"

"Jes a drank. Ah mean, uh, jes' ah swaller." While she carried the child in her arms, she led John through the front door.

"Do ya have any lard er grease?" John asked.

"Shore I do, it's in the kitchen on the stove."

"I need ya to melt some, about a cup, but don't get it too hot."

He followed her into the kitchen, where she quickly walked to the stove. Her hands shook as she melted the grease in a pan, and poured it into a glass, as John had instructed. She handed it to him, and he placed a small amount on his wrist to check the temperature, he sat down in a chair at the kitchen table, took the child onto his lap and coaxed her to drink.

"That oughta work." John said. "Might be best to take 'er outside. That ought to be a-comin' back up direckly."

The child reached for her mother and began crying. *"Mommy, me sick."*

"Honey, I knowed yer sick. Please don't cry. Oh, God, please let 'er be all right," she pleaded, as she reached for her child. She carried her outside, and John walked out the door behind them.

The child began to gag, and the contents of her stomach spewed forth. While holding the child to her breast, the woman looked at John with relief.

"Thankee, Mister uh, thankee so much. Do ya reckon she'll be all right?"

"She's a li'l scared, but she oughta be fine."

"I'm so grateful ya come by, I didn't knowed what to do. I was on the back porch warshin' laundry, an' then I turned to pick up some more clothes to put 'em into the warshin' machine, when I noticed she was holdin' tha cup o' Clorox an' drank some before I could grab the cup. I was right scairt, 'n' I grabbed 'er into my arms an' ran fer help. I'll nary fergitcha Mister, uh...."

"Name's John Winters, Ma'am, an' I'm just glad I could help. Try 'n' keep the Clorox outta 'er reach," he suggested with a smile.

"I'm Ruby Jackson," she said nervously. "Thankee so much. Ya saved 'er life. I shore will keep it outta her reach from now on. Uh, I done heered about you. Ain'tcha the pastor down at Mosey Grove Church? My mother goes to that church. Her name's Minnie Smith, a real sweet Christian woman that I love dearly. She shore brags about how much she likes yer preachin'. She always took me to church when I was growin' up, an' I figah I ought to start back a-goin' after this happenin'."

"I know, Sister Smith, an' she's a good Christian woman," he said. "Well, I oughta get back to work, an' I hope to see ya at church real soon." He turned to walk back to the road grader and finish his work for the day.

A man suddenly pushed the back door open. "Who in the hell is out heah?" He staggered out the door onto the porch.

"Be quiet, Ray, this here's Revrun Winters, the preacher down at Mosey Grove Church." Ruby spoke calmly, but appeared embarrassed.

"I ain't a wantin' no damn preacher at my house, an' I ain't a wantin no damn body a-talkin' to my wife." He spat as he spoke.

"Ray, Revrun Winters jes saved our baby's life, so will ya please jes go back to bed?" she pleaded.

John recognized from his red eyes and the sluggish look on his face, that he had been on a long drunk. He stepped closer to the porch and spoke in a caring tone, "Ray, Jesus loves ya, an' I'm shore yer wife loves ya too. I understand how you feel. I usta feel the same way you do 'bout church; an' I usta drank shine too, before I was saved. When I accepted the Lord into my life, was the best de-cision I ever made, for He is the only one who can help us overcome our weaknesses."

"Hell, I don't wanna talk about church, God er nothin', an' you kin jes leave, Mister Preacher-man, whatever yer name is." Ray stumbled backward. "I need another drank." He slurred his words as he staggered into the house and slammed the door with great force.

John waited patiently as he watched Ray stagger and nearly fall as he made his way into the house.

Ruby slowly bowed her head. "Revrun Winters, I'm so sorry 'bout Ray. He set up most the night lickered up. Evertime I ast 'im to go to church with me, he says he don't wanna hear about it, an' then he curses at me."

"Well, Missus Jackson, the best way to help yer husband is to pray for 'im, an' the good Lord'll take care of the rest. Prayer changes things. Believe me, I know. My wife prayed for me a long time before I seen the light and accepted the Lord as my personal Savior." He had a sparkle in his eyes and a smile on his lips as he spoke.

"Revrun, Winters, I knowed I need to start agoin to church an' straighten out my life. An' I knowed the only one who kin change my husband is God." She paused and looked at him with desperation in her eyes. "Please pray fer us, Revrun. I'm much obliged to ya fer helpin' Rachel I'll nary fergitcha."

"I shore will pray for you, an' your husband. An' I know another who's prayin' for ya too, a kind Christian woman who's a member of Mosey Grove Church," he added, as he smiled. Then he turned and walked away. He had deep sympathy for Ruby. He knew what an emotional battle she must be going through, living with a drunkard.

"I know who yer talkin 'bout, Revrun Winters," Ruby called out softly, as he walked away. "She done kept me in her prayers all my life."

John headed back to the road, where he had parked his road grader. He glanced back a final time, climbed into the driver's seat and drove slowly up the mountain. He had several hours left before the workday was over. As the road grader pushed slowly up the narrow road, John silently prayed that Ruby and Rachel would be all right and he prayed for the Lord to bless their home.

Ruby stood in her yard and watched John leave. Her mother's words echoed in her mind: *The Lord always sends the right person to help us in our time of need.* She looked up at the sky and thanked the Lord for sending Revrun Winters when he was needed.

She put the wiggling Rachel down to play, and walked up the porch steps into the kitchen, where she found Ray searching for another bottle of whiskey.

"Whar the hell's my bottle o' whiskey?"

"I don't know, Ray I think ya done drank it all last night."

"And who the damn hell invited the preacherman heah?" He stepped back and almost lost his balance.

"Ya tryin to git us to go to church agin? I done told ya, I hain't a-goin' to no damn church, I'm happy jes the way I am, an' I hain't a-goin' to change. He bes' nary come back heah no more!"

"I done told ya, Ray, he saved our baby's life." Ruby sniffled. "I was on the back porch a-warshin' clothes an' Rachel drank a swaller o' Clorox. I was so scairt. I dun't knowed what to do, an' I seen somebody on a road grader in front o' our house. I ran down to the road fer help, an' Revrun Winters come up to the house with me. He got 'er to drank a cup o' melted grease so she'd vomit. If it warnt fer Revrun Winters, Rachel might be dead," she explained, as a tear rolled down her cheek.

"Lans-sake, woman, ya need to keep a closer eye on 'er." He finally found a bottle of whiskey in the cabinet behind a bag of flour. He reached for the bottle and made his way to the bedroom. "Oh to hell with it! I'm a-goin' back to bed," he said, as he nearly fell through, the open doorway.

Ruby's heart was breaking as she stood quietly and watched her husband disappear into their bedroom. Rachel was crying softly. "It's okay, baby. Daddy's sick. We need to pray fer Daddy," Ruby whispered, as she choked back the tears.

John continued to grade the roads, one by one, as he worked his way across the mountain. With hard work and perspiration, he had tremendous determination to finish the job. After two weeks, and more than four miles of roads cleared, the job was finally completed.

Mr. Duncan then sent several trucks to dispense gravel over the roads. At long last, the school bus could drive across the mountain to pick up the children who lived in the area and take them to Coalfield School.

~~~~~~

The weeks slipped by quickly. The puppies were five months old, and each week John took them to the woods for a run. It wasn't long before they knew when it was time to go hunting. Training a foxhound can be a trying experience, and it takes a good trainer. John was an excellent trainer. He had a special way to call the dogs when he wanted them to return to him, using a "fox-horn" he had made by hand from a bull's horn that curved slightly upward. The horn was hollowed, with a hole at the smaller end. When calling the dogs, John placed his mouth over the opening and blew. Accustomed to the sound, the dogs returned immediately.

With remarkable endurance, wonderful senses of smell and strong desires to reach their quarry, they seemed to have been born with a special talent for tracking foxes. When they were on a fox trail, they knew how to "out-fox" the fox.

They learned quickly, and John planned to train them not only to hunt fox, but also wild hog. However, he wanted to teach them to fox hunt first. They followed commands extremely well.

John continued to use the foxtail drag technique he taught them earlier. Some drag hunts use a scented bag for such purpose, although sometimes the corpse of a fox is also used. John dragged the tail in various areas through the woods. Sometimes, he would skip to a different area to see if they could find the scent quickly.

Most of the time; Speed picked up the scent first. He seemed to enjoy the training procedure more than John did. While training the dogs, John found they taught each other hunting skills, as each would watch the other and listen closely when John gave a command, and then they tried to get the other to follow.

Fred stood 24 inches tall and weighed 65 pounds. He was lighter in color than Speed, with small black spots on his back. He had a long skull, soft brown eyes and two long brownish-red ears that, when pulled forward, almost touched his nose. His legs were straight and his paws were fox-like, with well-arched toes. He was full of energy, friendly and happy-go-lucky. In addition, he was a kind, loyal and lovable dog with a wonderful melodious bark that was pleasant to listen to, as if he were singing while on a chase.

John knew Speed was going to be larger than Fred was. He already stood 25 inches tall, and weighed 75 pounds. He had a long body with a long neck rising free, light from the shoulders, and he had a deep chest. His bark also had a melodious sound, but deeper than Fred's. He had black coloring on his back and around his ears, a medium-length coat and large brown eyes set far apart soft, and hound-like, with an expression gentle and pleading. His back was muscular and strong, with loins broad and slightly arched. Speed was obedient and eager to please his master, had a wonderful sense of smell and a strong-willed spirit, with more determination to stay on the fox's trail. This made him the lead dog.

~~~~~

With the advent of autumn, John decided to take the dogs on a real fox hunt. He recognized the fact that the dogs were ready and eager to go, and it was time for them to learn more about foxes. And Shane was eager to go hunting with his dad. John had taught his son great hunting skills. He often took Shane hunting on various occasions, when he was not busy with school work.

Some hunters say the fox enjoys the chase as much as the dog. During a chase, the fox can go underground and choose not to let the dog chase him; or, instead, play with the hound and maneuver its way through the woods leading the dog in circles. Hunting with a dog has the advantage of weeding out the sick and weak. The strongest foxes are most likely to escape and reproduce. They weigh 11 to 15 pounds and can run up to 30 miles per hour. A fox knows every inch of its territory by scent, and is alert and cunning. This is important, because they breed a litter of three to six pups, and live just four or five years. A fox can hear the call over a mile away. There is no point in whistling a fox during breeding season. They will not come. A fox can be a cunning animal, but can also be quite stupid. If the foxhound is alert and well trained, he can skillfully over take the fox. If hunting fox for their pelts, it is best to hunt them in the winter months, when they are at their best. Their fur is thicker and richer in color at such time.

John called on his friends Bill Watson and Joe Brown to bring their dogs, too. Bill had two dogs, Black and Blue. Joe had one dog named Baby Doll, a good female foxhound.

They gathered their dogs and their 20-gauge shotguns and drove a mile into a wooded area behind Joe's house. John thought hunting with other dogs would help Fred and Speed's hunting skills.

They got out of the truck and let the dogs loose. John began calling the fox, by whistling with a series of loud, piercing shrieks that imitated a wounded rabbit; then he reduced it to a low wailing sound as though the rabbit were defenseless. He waited several minutes before continuing the call, so that the fox would not be suspicious.

The five dogs started over the ridge, and Bill's dog Blue picked up a scent. Fred and Speed were directly behind him.

John's eyes opened wide and he exclaimed in excitement. "Yeah! Look at my dawgs right behind ol' Blue. They're catching on to fox-huntin' real fast."

"Listen at Baby Doll. She's a-keepin' right with 'em. 'Em dawgs are a-runnin' like the wind, an' closin' in on that ol' fox," Joe said, as he picked up his pace.

"Why, listen at 'em barkin'. It sounds like music to my ears. He cupped his hand over his ear and listened. Them dawgs are a-runnin' up the ridge right on the fox's trail. He may as well give it up. That ol' fox ain't got a chance," John proclaimed.

Looking rather pleased, Bill said, "I hear Black 'n' Blue right with 'im. All the dawgs are stayin' right together."

"Yup, now, ol' Speed is in the lead, I can tell his bark anywhars," John said. "Yessir, 'em two dawgs are some fine huntin' dawgs. Dan Jackson offered to buy 'em from me. Lemme tell ya, I wouldn't sell my dawgs for any amount of money; I care about 'em dawgs more'n any dawgs I ever owned. I've been teachin' Fred 'n' Speed to hunt ever week since they were two months ol'. They been together all their lives an' I'm aimin' to keep 'em that way always."

"That's the way I feel about Baby Doll. I got 'er when she was a pup, an' she's three years old now. Boys, a fella kin shore get attached to his dawg," Joe added, trying to catch up with John.

Bill raised his brow and laughed. "Yep! Hain't that the truth? Sometimes yer dawg's more loyal than yer ol' lady."

"Bill, ya got a good woman, an' ya knowed it," John said, walking a bit faster.

"I know. I wouldn't trade 'er fer the world." Bill laughed.

"C'mon, Shane, try to keep up."

"Don't worry, Daddy. I'm right behind ya." He answered.

"C'mon, I hear 'em runnin up the hill over yonder, we don't wanna lose our dawgs," Joe added.

The four men ran through briers and thick brush. When they reached the top of the hill, John cupped his hand over his ear. "Listen, Speed's still in the lead an' the other dawgs are stayin' right with 'im." He continued listening. "Sounds like the fox is backtrackin an' bringin' the dawgs back this-a-way."

"Yeah, yer right, John. Sounds like that ol' fox is a-playin' with our dawgs," Bill said with a laugh.

"Well, we'll be ready fer 'im," Joe added. "I jes got this here new 20-gauge shotgun. I traded Thomas Hall a cow from my herd fer it. Sam wanted a cow so's he'd have meat fer the winter, on accounta, ya know ol' Sam don't do much huntin'. This ol' gun shore shoots good. I got my sight set jes right. If that fox comes this way, fellas, I'll get 'im."

The three men stood quietly listening to determine the direction the dogs were running. After a while, John heard the dogs barking, and, by the sound of it, they were running straight toward them. He stood with his shotgun ready, listening to the barking of the dogs, as it grew increasingly loud and close.

Shane stood watching their every move, determined to become a skilled hunter like his dad.

The men raised their guns. "Get ready. That fox is a-runnin right at us. He might pop up outta nowhars." John said.

They continued to stand very quietly, listening. The dogs were closing in on the fox and making rapid strides. Without further warning, the fox jumped up from a thicket 40 feet away. Joe raised his gun to take a shot.

BANG!

He missed. The fox continued to run, and the men called the dogs back, to stop for the day.

"Sorry, ya missed him, Joe. Them dawgs gave that fox a durn good run," Bill said with a smile.

"Well, he caught us by surprise. He just darted out from the bushes," John said, half-defending Joe's shot.

"Sometimes, ya gotta to aim a-might fast to kill a fox," Joe said, shaking his head.

"It's just about dark, an' my belly's as hollow as an ol' burnt-out stump. Shane, we'd best head back home. I hope ya mama saved us some supper," John said, forgetting the miss.

"That's a dandy idée. Let's get the dogs back into the truck an' head on back home. We'll try 'n' go huntin' agin in a week er two," Bill said.

The sun was setting behind the mountain and darkness was approaching. John drove home slowly and arrived just after dark. John and Shane walked quietly into the kitchen and found two plates of food in the oven. Rosie knew they wouldn't make it home in time for supper. Waiting for them was fried chicken, mashed potatoes, green beans and cornbread. The two sat at the kitchen table and enjoyed their food and the quiet evening.

Afterward, John went outside to feed his dogs and give them water, so they could bed down for the night. He did not have to tell Shane to go to bed. The long day of hunting had taken its toil on his body.

Before going to bed, John walked into the sitting room to his favorite chair. *Time for a moment with my Lord,* he thought. He opened his Bible to the book of Proverbs and read for 30 minutes. He gave thanks for the blessings in his life, especially the greatest ones in the nearby bedrooms asleep in their beds. He let the love of the Lord comfort his soul. He realized he was sleepier than he had thought, and he gently laid the Bible on the table beside him, stood up, and went to bed.

~~ Chapter Five ~~

One cool November evening, John drove to Bill Watson's house to see if he wanted to go hog hunting in the Catoosa Wildlife Area. He thought it best for Shane not to go on the hunting trip, due to the danger of hunting wild boar. The Catoosa hunting area covers over 82,000 acres in Cumberland and Morgan counties. The land has some of the most rugged terrain in the country, with many trails for hiking. The most notable is the Cumberland Trail. Included among wildlife in the area are: deer, squirrel, rabbit, boar, turkey and various small animals.

John pulled his truck into Bill's driveway and stopped near the front porch. Bill opened the front door and called, "C'mon in, John. Make yerself right at home."

"I don't aim to stay long. I just stopped by to see if you'd go hawg huntin' next week in Catoosy. I already talked to Joe, an' he's game. My dawgs are gettin' restless an' they're a-wantin' to go huntin' again. I ain't been on a wild hawg hunt in a coon's age."

"Shore, John, I'll get my dawgs ready to go. Maybe I can get my wife to pack us some dinner, for we're gonna be in the woods all day."

"Okay, Bill, see ya next week. I best get on back home, it's a-gettin' late."

The next week rolled around quickly, and Fred and Speed could sense the excitement in John. He fed the dogs a large meal the night before the hunt. He knew they would need energy if they were going to bay a wild boar. John got up at 4 a.m. He wanted to get into the Catoosa area early, before the hog's eyesight improved with daylight.

The temperature was cold, and John dressed in a pair of thick pants over his long johns, a blue plaid, flannel shirt, a worn pair of brown boots and his favorite blue cap. After he put on his jacket and grabbed his 12-gauge shotgun, he loaded the dogs into the back of his panel truck. He picked up Bill and his two dogs, Black, and Blue, then headed to Joe's house for him and for his dog, Baby Doll. She had a sweet, humble personality and soft brown eyes that could melt one's heart.

En route to the Catoosa area, John remarked, "The area whar we're huntin' is full o' wild hawg, so it won't take us long to find some sign, onest we get in thar. They leave slashes on trees from their tusks to mark their territory. The higher up, the bigger the hawg."

"Yeah, you kin also look fer the place whar they leave signs on the ground from wallowin' to make beddin' areas," Joe added.

"Fellas, nothin's more thrillin' than for a man to be faced with a 200- to 400-pound mean ol' nasty bayed wild hawg. An' my two dawgs shore knows how to bay a hawg," Bill said proudly.

"Onest ya go through a good hawg hunt, that's sump'n ya hain't likely ta fergit, an' yer addicted fer life," Joe said.

John laughed. "Yeah, wild hawgs are challengin' animal to hunt. It's best to try 'n' stay down wind if ya can, on accounta their keen sense o' smell."

"The dad-burned things are built like army tanks, but it can be a clean kill if ya hit it in the right spot with a big enough shotgun," Bill said. "But it'll come after ya if ye only hurt it."

"If you ever seen 'em use them razor-sharp tusks ta uproot food, you knowed they kin easily rip a fella er a animal wide open," Joe said.

They reached the Catoosa area and found a spot to park. The woods were thick with trees and brush, and they had to leave the truck and walk the rest of the way.

The three men got out of the truck with their shotguns and let the dogs loose.

A little over a mile in, John saw evidence of a boar. "A big hawg's close by. See whar he's been markin' his territry? Be on the lookout."

"Yeah, keep yer eyes peeled. It's pert-near daylight. I hain't wantin' that ol' hawg havin' us fer breakfus!" Joe added.

"Ya, reckon ya could out run a hawg?" Bill laughed as he spoke.

"Naw, but I got me a good shotgun I kin shoot him with," Joe joked back.

They continued walking a couple more miles, when they stopped to rest by a large oak tree, leaning their guns against a smaller tree nearby. Bill and Joe had just sat down on a log and John placed his hand against the oak tree and leaned back to rest.

BANG!

It came from one of the shotguns that had fallen from its position where it was leaning. The blast strunk John's right foot. He fell to the ground in excruciating pain.

When he saw John fall, Bill leaped to his feet and shouted, "John, yer foot's been shot."

In shock, and shaking all over, Joe cried out, "What do we do? Oh! What do we do?"

"Take yer belt off, Bill, an' tie it around my calf, er I'll bleed to death." John said.

Bill yanked off his belt and secured it tightly around John's leg, as his hands shook, and his face was etched with worry. "We aim to get you to a hospital. Both of us can help gitcha to the truck."

"I don't know if I can hop on one laig that far. It's about three miles back to the road." John reached into his coat pocket and brought forth a bottle of Anacin tablets. He barely got the lid opened, poured six pills into his shaky hand, and popped them into his mouth.

Tilting his head back, he choked the pills down, hoping they would lessen the agonizing pain. "Don't leave me."

"Now hush that kinda talk, John, we hain't gonna leave ya. You can make it. Just lean on us an' we'll help ya," Bill promised, and Joe agreed.

They got on either side of John so that he could put his arms around their necks for support. It took both men to get John up on his one good foot. He was a big man. Bill and Joe were smaller than John, but together, they were able to assist him as he hopped on his left foot.

"Hey, Bill, what about our sack an' the guns? It's gonna be hard ta tote our guns an' hep 'im outta here," Joe said.

"Just leave the sack. We gotta bring our guns. We can carry 'em on our backs. We don't wanna be out here an' that hawg sneak up on us," Bill replied.

John struggled to hop on his left leg, with the help of his friends, for a half mile. "I got to rest just a minute. My foot is numb an' my laig is throbbin'." He looked down, "It looks like the belt is holdin' it, but it's still bleedin' some." He saw that his pant leg was soaked with blood. The men helped him sit on the ground, against a pine tree, to rest for ten minutes.

"I plum fergot 'bout the dawgs." Joe remarked.

"Don't worry none about the dawgs, they're right behind us. They can find their way outta the woods," Bill said.

Just after Bill's remark, the dogs ran up the hill toward them. They heard the gun discharge from the other ridge, and came back to see what had happened.

Fred and Speed knew John was hurt. They could smell the blood, and Speed came closer to greet him. John rubbed Speed's head, "I'll be okay boy, if I can make it outta here." Fred started to whimper, as if he were crying.

"C'mon, fellas, help me up, an' let's try to go a bit further," John said in a voice displaying his pain.

There was a mile to go before they reached the road, and it was two hours since the accident. John became weaker with each passing moment.

"Oh! I gotta stop again, just for a minute. Oh, Lord, am I gonna make it? Please help me, Lord," John cried out.

"Yer gonna make it, John. If it's the Good Lord's will, you'll make it outta here," Bill said, trying to encourage. John's breath was shallow and slow.

John looked at him. "Yeah, yer right, Bill, the Lord's never lemme down. We still got nearly a mile to go. Let's try 'n' go a bit further."

He struggled, desperately, trying to be strong but failing, as they made their way over a hill. In a shaky voice, he said, "I'm gettin' weak. I don't know if I can make it." He began to pray aloud. *"Lord, please don't lemme die out here in these woods an' leave my wife 'n' childrun. Not now, Lord."* He paused, and took a deep breath. "It's been three hours, an' I don't know how much blood I've lost. I cain't feel my foot anymore, an' my laig is on fahr. I ain't got much strenth left, an'…, uh…, an' I'm a-feelin' woozy."

"Don'tcha be passin' out on us John, er we'll never gitcha outta here," Joe said nervously. John looked extraordinarily pale.

"Joe, I'm tryin'. The road…, oughta be…, just over that hill. I gotta make it," John said. His voice began to fade.

"Lean on us an' we'll gitcha to the other side o' that hill. Then it's just a li'l way to the road." Bill said.

Joe looked at Bill and whispered, "He's a-gettin' weaker, an' he's a-havin' trouble breathin'. The road bes' be just ahead, or he hain't gonna make it."

"I cain't hop-much-further."

"Shhh. Don't talk no more, John. Save yer energy," Bill said.

The dogs continued to follow behind them. Bill and Joe helped John to balance himself as they worked their way down the hill.

Bill looked up. "I think I see the road just ahead."

When at last they reached the road, Bill glanced around disappointed, "We come out on the road just north o' whar we parked. The truck is a half mile down."

"Oh, Lord! What're we gonna do?" John really sounded scared. "I'm so weak, I'll never make it to the truck. Everthin' looks blurry. I think I'm gonna fall out." As he spoke, his good leg buckled under him and he began to collapse. It took all of Bill's strength to cushion his fall.

"Wait! I hear sump'n a-comin'," Joe said desperately. An old black pickup truck came into view with a man in his fifties behind the wheel. Joe waved his arms for the man to stop.

The driver saw John lying on the ground, and noted the blood on his clothing, knew he was injured. He quickly pulled to the side of the road and stopped.

"Please, Mister," Bill pleaded. "Can ya get us to a hospital? He done lost alot a blood."

"Shore, get him on in the truck and lay 'im down in the back. I'll drive ya to Harriman Hospital. It's about 25 miles away. He jumped out of the truck. "Lemme help ye with 'im," the man offered. The three men lifted John onto the bed of the truck.

"Bill, ya go on with 'im to the hospital, an' I'll drive his panel truck back to his house," Joe said. "I'll take the dawgs on home, tell his wife about the accident, an' let her know John's in Harriman. Then, I'll take yer two dawgs to my house an' ya kin pick 'em up later. Besides, I need to get on back home di-reckly. My wife hain't been feelin' well lately. Her sister, Edith, is stayin' with 'er 'til I get home."

"Okay, Joe, let Rosie know we're goin' to Harriman Hospital."

Joe put all the dogs into the back of the panel truck and drove to John's house.

Bill sat on the truck bed with John, while the man drove to the hospital. After 15 minutes, John opened his eyes. "I feel so weak," he said, then he closed his eyes again.

"Just lay still, John, yer on the way to the hospital."

The drive took 30 minutes. The road to Harriman was extremely winding, and mostly gravel. The hospital was a small facility with one floor, 50 beds and two large rooms for emergency. It was staffed by 300 employees and 12 doctors on call.

When they arrived, Bill leaped out of the back of the truck, rushed into the emergency room, and shouted, "Help me! Bring a bed or wheelchair. Thar's a fella outside that's been shot."

An ambulance driver and a nurse were working in ER and brought John into the hospital on a stretcher. Bill walked outside and returned to the stranger who drove them to the hospital. "Much obliged for yer kindness. I'm sorry, I didn't gitcher name. I'm Bill Watson, an' my friend is John Winters."

"Nice to meetcha, Mister Watson, I reckon through all the commotion, I forgot to innerduce my ownself, too. Name's Randall Whitaker. Just glad I could help. I hope he'll be all right." After saying goodbye, Mr. Whitaker drove away.

Dr. Simpson was working in ER. He was a tall, slender man, in his late 40s, with brown eyes and black hair, graying at the temples. He could see that the gunshot wound was serious, and John was enormously pale from losing so much blood. The doctor ordered pain medication and an IV, and he told the nurse to get John's blood type so he could start a unit of blood. Next, the doctor ordered an X-ray of his foot.

When the doctor left the room, John lay on a narrow bed and stared at the ceiling. His body felt weak and cold. His foot had turned dark from lack of blood flow. His entire body was trembling, and he felt all alone. The day was a nightmare, and he hoped he would waken from it soon. As he tried to block out the throbbing pain in his leg, he closed his eyes to pray:

I come to ya Lord with a humble heart. I ast ya to help me with this awful tragedy. I cain't face this alone, Lord, for my heart is heavy with sorrah. You said in yer Word that you'd never leave us nor forsake us. I know yer all powerful, Lord, an' can hear yer childrun when they call on ya. Yer my shelter in times o' storm, the rock I build my faith on, an' the Savior of my soul. I ast ya, Lord, to gimme strength to face what lies ahead. Please, help me, Lord, an' watch over my family. In Jesus name, I pray. Amen.

After a short while, Dr. Simpson got the test results and studied the film carefully. Twenty minutes later he walked into John's room to explain the test results. "Mr. Winters, your foot and ankle bone have far too much damage to repair. In addition, the foot has been without blood for so long, gangrene has set in and infection too serious to treat. Your foot will have to be amputated about eight inches below the knee. It's the only option to save your life. We'll fit you with an artificial leg and get you into therapy."

"No, doc, ya cain't cut off my laig. My wife ought to be on the way down here. Just wait 'til my wife gets here."

Dr. Simpson frowned. "Okay, Mr. Winters, we'll wait awhile, until your wife gets here."

As the doctor left, Bill entered the room. "What'd the doctor say? Can they save yer foot?"

John frowned. "They say no, Bill. My foot and part o' my laig gotta come off. I don't want 'em to take my laig off. I'm a-waitin' for Rosie. She'll prob'ly get Clifford Jones to bring 'er. She should be here direckly." He paused. "Bill, this is the hardest thing I ever had to face."

~~~~~~

Joe arrived at John's home. He drove the truck up the small hill leading to the house, stopped 20 feet from the front door and got out of the truck to open the back panel doors and release John's dogs. He kept Bill's two dogs and his dog, Baby Doll, in the back while he went into the house to tell Rosie about the accident. Fred and Speed jumped out and ran behind the house to see if they could find food. Joe heard laughter coming from inside as he walked closer to the house, and he knocked loudly on the front door.

Ellie opened the door. "Is Rosie home?" Joe asked.

Lula, standing next to Ellie, looked up at Joe.

"Whar's my daddy?"

"Yer daddy'll be home later, honey."

"You drove my daddy's truck home. Whar's Daddy?" Ellie asked.

"Yeah, honey, I drove yer daddy's truck. He'll be home later. Is yer mama home?"

"Joe, I'm in the kitchen. C'mon in," Rosie called.

Neva sat quietly on the couch and watched as Joe made his way to Rosie. When Joe entered the kitchen, Rosie saw the blood on his pants, and, by the expression on his face, she knew something was terribly wrong.

"Rosie, I hate ta tell ya this, but John got shot in the foot, an' I think his ankle bone is shattered." Sorrow was reflected in Joe's eyes.

Rosie's voice quivered as she held back the tears. "Whar's he at? Is he all right?"

Joe swallowed. He was nervous. "Yeah," he responded. "He's gone to the Harriman Hospital. It took us pert-near four hours ta get him outta them woods, an' this fella come along the road in an ol' pickup truck an' drove John to the hospital. Bill went with 'im, an' I drove John's truck ta bring the dawgs back on home."

"I gotta get to the hospital 'n' see 'im. The kids can stay here. Becky's 14 now. She's old enuff to watch 'em. Shane's gone to a friend's house to stay all night."

"John wanted ya to get somebody else ta take ya to the hospital, seein' as I ain't got no drivin' license right now, an' all these dawgs are in the truck. I was worried about drivin' the truck back here. I don't like ta drive in a city if I don't gotta. I lost my license, an' I nary did go get me another'n."

"Don't worry about it none, Joe, I'll get our neighbor, Clifford, to drive me thar. You go on ahead 'n' take John's truck home. You can bring it back later."

"Thankee, Rosie. Now ya tell John not ta fret much, an' I'll come 'n' see him in a day er two. I got ta get on home before dark. My wife's been sick. Doc said 'twas some kinda heart disease, an' she got the high blood pressure. I'll be seein' ya, Rosie."

"Bye, Joe. Give yer wife my best.

Rebecca, come here!" Rosie shouted.

Becky and Laura were in their bedroom talking when they heard their mother call. They ran into the kitchen to learn what was wrong. "Yes, Mama, what's wrong? You never call me Rebecca 'less yer upset," she said, as she frowned. She could see that something bad must have happened. Tears were in her mother's eyes.

Rosie hesitated, and then spoke carefully. "Your daddy's been in an accident today an' was shot in the foot. Joe told me it shattered his foot an' shot out his anklebone. You 'n' Laura watch the kids 'til I get back from the hospital."

"Is he gonna be all right, Mama?" Becky asked, as eyes filled with tears.

"We wanna go with ya," Laura said.

"Please, Mama, can we go?" Ellie asked.

"No. Y'uns stay here. Becky, run on over to the Jones an ask Clifford if he'll drive me to Harriman Hospital."

"Yes, Mama, I'll hurry fast as I can."

Ten minutes later, Clifford pulled up at John's house, with Becky sitting beside him. She got out as Rosie approached the car.

"You kids be good an' mind Becky, I'll be back sometime tomorrah if I can." She got into Clifford's car and closed the door.

"Becky told me John got shot. What happen?" Clifford asked.

Rosie took a deep breath. "Joe drove the truck back from the huntin' trip with the dawgs, an' told me John got shot in the foot an' his ankle bone is shattered. Bill went with him to the hospital."

"Now try 'n' not worry, Rosie. The doctors at the hospital will take good care of 'im. I'm shore John'll be jes fine. And ah don't mind one li'l bit drivin' ya ta Harriman. Ah think a lot o' you 'n' John. Y'all done been good neighbors ta me 'n' my famly. I'll do anythin' ah kin fer ya. Jes' lemme know."

The drive down the mountain seemed to take longer than usual. Rosie couldn't help but worry, as a million thoughts rushed through her mind.

In time, they arrived at the hospital. They walked through the front entrance, approached the front desk, and asked directions to John's room. After giving Rosie directions, the nurse told her Dr. Simpson wished to talk with her. After the doctor explained the diagnosis to her, Rosie walked into John's room and saw the pain on his face. She rushed to his bedside, leaned over and put her arms around him.

John wrapped his arms around her and pleaded, "Don't let 'em take my laig off, Rosie, I cain't lose my laig."

A tear rolled down his cheek. As they embraced she felt him tremble. She began to cry, and when she looked into his saddened face, she felt her heart broken. The look in his eyes spoke louder than words. He was frightened.

"I don't know if I can do it, Rosie. I cain't lose my laig."

"John, the doctor talked to me just before I came to see ya. He said it was the only thing he could do to save yer life. And I don't wanna lose ya, honey." She tried in vain to stop the tears.

The door opened. "Mr. Winters, we need to operate soon," Dr. Simpson said, looking concerned.

Worried, John glanced at Rosie, and then looked at the doctor. "Well, Doc, if that's the only thing ya can do."

A few minutes later, two nurses came into the room to take John into surgery. As he was being wheeled out, Rosie stopped the gurney, kissed him on the cheek and whispered into his ear, *"The Lord will take good care of ya. Don't be afraid. I'll be a prayin for ya."*

~~ Chapter Six ~~

Bill and Rosie were sitting in the waiting room. They hadn't spoken for several minutes. Bill looked at her. "I know this here's gonna be powerful hard on you 'n' John, an alot a times we question the Lord when things like this happen."

"I know, Bill. It takes great effort to keep yer faith at a time like this. I keep askin' God, "Why John?" She placed her hands over her face and began to sob.

Bill laid his hand on her back to comfort her. "I understand, Rosie, an' sometimes, when tragedy enters our lives, even strong faith can falter." He cleared his throat and continued, "I don't like to talk none about this, but when my first young-un was borned, the baby lived for about ten minutes an' then died. The baby was a boy.

For a short while, I hated God for takin' my son from me."

"Oh, Bill, I'm so sorry to hear aboutcher baby. We don't always understand the trials 'n' tribulations that we have to go through, but I know God does love us," she said, through her tears.

"I know, Rosie. When the baby died, my wife had a deeper hurt than I did, but her strength helped me to accept it. It took a while to believe in the Lord agin an' get my faith back. Then I realized, one day I'll see my son again. I knowed I don't fully understand it now, but I'll understand it in the sweet by-n-by, when this life's over." He paused. "Rosie, yer faith has always been strong in the Lord. Yer the kindest an' strongest woman I knowed," He gently took her hand in his. "If you er John needs anything er needs help in any way, jes lemme know. He's the bes' friend I ever had."

Rosie wiped her nose on a tissue and sighed. "John feels the same way 'bout you, an' I know somehow the Lord'll help us through this. And, Bill, I, too, understand what yer talkin' about. Our first two babies were taken from us a few minutes after birth. It took a long time for me to accept it an' realize God knows best."

They had been waiting more than two hours, when Dr. Simpson came into the waiting room. "Mrs. Winters? Your husband came through the surgery just fine. It will be a while before he wakes up. He'll need to stay in the hospital about two weeks, and then it will take about two months for his leg to heal. We need to wait until his leg shrinks before it will fit an artificial leg properly."

"Thankee, doctor. When can I see him?"

"The nurse will let you know when he comes out of recovery, Mrs. Winters." The doctor then turned and left.

Rosie was relieved, but drained from waiting and worrying. Several minutes had passed, and, while lost in her thoughts, the nurse startled her. "Mrs. Winters, you can see your husband now, but just for a few minutes. He'll be in recovery for two or three hours, 'n' then we'll move him to ICU for a couple o' days."

She slowly stood to follow the nurse. "I 'preciate it. Excuse me, Bill, I'll be back in a few minutes."

She entered through double doors and looked at John in the quiet room. She could hear his heart beat through the monitor. Several tubes were attached to him, and he was extremely pale. She stood quietly for several moments looking at him.

The nurse walked to the other side of the bed. "Mr. Winters lost a lot o' blood. We give him three units in the OR." She held a needle in her hand as she rolled John to one side. "This here for pain," she said, as she injected the medication into his hip. "You can stay for about ten minutes, an' then you got to return to the waitin' area. I'll letcha know when we take 'im to ICU."

"Thankee, nurse. I won't stay but a few minutes." A tear rolled down her face. She sat by John's bedside in silence, looking at the kind, handsome face she fell in love with. He was her knight in shining armor in times of trouble; he was the one person who made her feel complete; the person who filled her heart with love. She knew she would have difficulty living without him.

She rose, slowly walked back to the waiting area and sat beside Bill. "He lost a lot o' blood, and they give 'im a shot for pain. I knowed ya need to get on home. I'll never be able to thankee enough for everthin' ya done for John." She took a long breath. "I'll stay all night an' get Clifford to take me on home tomorrah to check on the kids. He said he would drivin' back down here tomorrah, anyway."

"Rosie, I'm glad he's gonna be all right." He relaxed a little. "I do need to get on home and get out of these dirty clothes. Just lemme know if I can do anythin' for you er John." he said, with sympathy.

After Bill left, Rosie remained in the waiting area, praying for John and thinking about their lives together. She stared bleary-eyed out the window, and each minute felt like an eternity. She placed her trembling hands together, closed her eyes and prayed:

Dear Lord, please help me an' gimme the faith an' the strenth I need to accept what lies ahead. I ast ya, Lord, to give John the strength he needs to get through this. I know I failed ya many times, Lord, but ya always been there for me. Lord, you've reached down many times an' picked me up. Evertime I call upon ya, Lord, yer always nearby. I thank ya, Lord, that John is still alive, an' you didn't take him from me. Please touch my husband, Lord, an' heal his body. I ast this in Jesus' holy sweet name. Amen.

Unaware what the future might bring, she placed her faith in God. She opened her heart, longing to feel His gentle touch. She desperately tried to place her trust in the Lord. She sensed her anguish lift, and she felt complete comfort in the shelter of His arms. For a moment, she sat in silence, and allowed the peacefulness of the Holy Spirit to fill her soul.

A nurse came into the waiting area and, in a tender voice addressed her. "Mrs. Winters, your husband is now in ICU. You can see him for 15 minutes."

"Thankee," Rosie eagerly replied, and she anxiously walked down the hallway to ICU. As she came closer to John's bed, she watched as he tried to open his eyes. It was hard to focus on his face as tears again filled her eyes. She took John's hand in hers. "John can ya hear me? I'm right here. Don'tcha worry, your gonna be all right."

He opened his eyes for a few seconds and smiled at her. Her presence put him at ease. She sat with him until he dozed off again, and she kissed him on the cheek, got up and returned to the waiting room.

Shortly before dawn, she fell asleep and slept for two hours. She wakened and her head nodded, and she sat slumped over, for a time. Her body ached from sitting in the same position for so long. She sat up straight in her chair feeling sluggish, yawned, opened her eyes wider, and ran her fingers through her hair, trying to look presentable as she faced a new day.

The room remained quiet. She glanced at the wall clock and found the time was 6:35 a.m. Visitation for ICU began at 7 a.m. With nothing to do but think, she recalled special moments during her marriage. The memories made her smile. Her thoughts took her back to the day they were married, and she realized that during their marriage there were many more good times than bad.

Their wedding day, Christmas Eve, 1936: *The day was vividly clear in her mind. They were so deeply in love, nothing else mattered. With her spirit high and filled with joy, she felt her life was perfect.*

John had a close friend, Reverend Jonathan Miles, who lived in Wartburg, where he owned a hardware store. Reverend Miles married John's parents and John wanted the reverend to marry them. The wedding was at the reverend's home. The three folks who attended the wedding were Reverend Miles, his wife, Ester; and Hanna, their granddaughter.

After the wedding, they went on a buggy ride, deep into the woods to a small cabin, where they spent their first night together, and their first Christmas.

Rosie recalled it perfectly. *She was extremely nervous. However, the gentle way John held her made her feel secure and relaxed in his arms. As they lay in bed, with moonlight softly illuminating the room, he slid his fingers down her back, exploring the softness of her skin, and whispered, "Rosie, ya make me complete."*

She replied, in a soft whisper, as she brought him closer to her breast, "I love ya, John."

"I love ya, too, Rosie," he said passionately. As he covered his mouth with hers, they drifted into another world. A tingling sensation ran up her back as he kissed her, and it gave her a great desire to melt in his arms. Their hearts wove together, and she, filled with love, clung to his body.

A sweet melody played in her heart. Every beat was in rhythm with his. The night air was electric. As their bodies joined, their passion grew. They flew to the highest level, and came down in satisfaction, completing the circle of love. The night was perfect, and would remain in her memory forever.

She often thought of that enchanting night, and the magic of Christmas. She smiled, as she had many fond memories of their life together. She was in such deep thought; she jumped as the nurse walked into the room.

"Mrs. Winters, its 7 a.m., visitation time for ICU. You can see your husband now."

"Thankee." She stood up and followed the nurse down the hallway, through double doors and into ICU. John slowly opened his eyes and smiled at her as she approached his bedside, although he couldn't hide his heavily burdened heart from her. She smiled and took his hand in hers. "I love ya, John."

"I love ya too, Rosie. I know this'll be a big burden on ya." He looked worried.

"Now, John, don'tcha say that. I'm so grateful yer still alive. Nothin' could be worser than losin' ya."

"How am I gonna take care of my family with just one laig?" He asked.

Her fingers trembled as she gently touched his face. "We'll manage somehow, John. God always provides. He's carried us through many a trial. The Lord always has something good come from something bad. I know ya cain't see the good now, but everthin'll work out. You'll see."

"I get so much strenth from ya, Rosie." he said, as he looked into her eyes.

"And you gimme joy 'n' happiness," she said, as she brushed his hair back from his forehead. She smiled at him and continued. "The doctor was a-talkin' to me yesterday about a company in Knoxv'lle that can fitcha with a laig. You'll be fine, John. It's just gonna take some time."

The nurse brought a food tray, and smiled at her caringly. "Mrs. Winters, I don't mean to interrupt none, but here's some breakfast. They brung an extra tray an' I knowed you hadn't ate since yesterday. You're welcome to it."

"I'm much obliged, nurse. I might try an' eat a li'l. It's right kind of ya bein' so thoughtful. Everybody at the hospital's treated us so nice, an' I thankee for everthin' yer doin for my husband."

"Your more'n welcome, Mrs. Winters," the nurse answered, as she turned to check on other patients.

Later, the nurse smiled and said, "Mrs. Winters, I'm sorry, but visitin' time's up. You can go back to the waitin' room, and if there's any change, I'll letcha know."

"Okay. Thankee, nurse," Rosie said. "I'll see ya after while. I love ya, John."

"I love ya, too, Rosie," John said, as he kissed her goodbye.

As Rosie slid into a chair in the waiting room, Clifford arrived.

"How's he doin', Rosie?"

"A li'l better today, Clifford. His blood pressure's under control an' his color's a-comin' back." She let out a sigh of relief. "I need to get on back home for awhile an' check on my young-uns."

"That's the reason Ah come down, ta check on John an' see if yer aimin' fer me to drive ya back home."

"I don't know how to thankee, Clifford for all you've done, drivin' me back 'n' forth to the hospital."

"Rosie, why you know I'd help you er John any way ah can."

"I know, Clifford." She slowly stood up, feeling exhausted. "I'll go 'n' say bye to John, an' tell him I'm goin' home."

She returned shortly. "Okay Clifford, I reckon I'm ready to go, if you are."

~~~~~~

It was early afternoon when Rosie arrived home. The three youngest children were playing outside; Becky and Laura were in the kitchen doing dishes; and Shane was in the back yard feeding the dogs. As she got out of the car, the three in the yard ran to hug her, eager to learn about their daddy.

"You young-uns best get in the house. It's a gettin' cold out here."

"We ain't cold, Mama. We'll go in the house in a minute. How's Daddy? Can we go see him?" Ellie asked.

Neva ran to her mother, wrapped her arms around her leg and looked up with her big, brown eyes. "I wanna see Daddy."

"Yer daddy's just fine, Li'l Indian. He's in the hospital. He'll be a-comin' home di-reckly."

Lula begged, "Cain't we go to the hospital?"

"Now ya know yer too young to go in the hospital. Ya kids have to stay here. Yer daddy'll come home in about two weeks."

As Rosie entered the kitchen, Becky stopped washing dishes and came over to give her a comforting hug. Rosie could see the hurt in Becky's eyes before she started crying. "Did they cut Daddy's foot off, Mama?"

Rosie hesitated, as a lump formed in her throat. "Yes, they did, Becky, an' when he gets well, we can get him an artificial laig. The doctor said he'll be fine. He just gotta get usta his new laig. It's gonna take time, Becky."

She turned and saw Shane standing just inside the kitchen, at the back door. He had heard the conversation. Without a word, he opened the door leading up to the loft and made his way to his bedroom. Laura didn't speak, but continued to wash dishes, with tears in her eyes.

Rosie knew, with God's help, the family would get through the tragedy. She always put her trust in Him in times of need. She drew her strength from the Lord, and from the family she loved so deeply. Her children were the anchor in her life and her sense of purpose.

~~~~~

Later, she decided it would be best to find someone to look after the kids while she was staying at the hospital for the next couple of weeks. She walked to her neighbor, Mrs. Annie Galloway's house, a quarter mile away. Mrs. Galloway was a kind Christian woman who was always willing to help. She was in her late fifties, with dark brown hair and light gray highlights, which she wore in a bun on top of her head. She continually worked in her house or in her garden, and was very strong for her age, yet she always had energy to spare.

Rosie walked to the front door and knocked. Annie opened the door she smiled and said, "Well, lookie thar! Rosie Winters. I hain't seen ya in a month o' Sundys. How ya been doin'? Come in and make yerself right to home."

"Good to see ya again, Annie. I don't aim to stay long. I just come to see if ya'd stay with my young-uns until John gets outta the hospital. I guess ya heard about his huntin' accident?"

"Lawdy, how awful. How's he doin'?"

"He seemed to be doin' better when I left the hospital this mornin'. It's hard for him to accept losin' his laig. I was wonderin' if ya'd come to the house tomorrah mornin' an stay with the kids. Clifford is gonna drive me back to Harriman again."

"Why, you knowed I'd be happy to watch after them young-uns whilst yer at the hospital with Revrun Winters."

Annie always enjoyed Rosie's company or the children coming to visit her. Not surprisingly, when the children came to visit she always had a fresh batch of peanut butter cookies. She had no children at home, as her two daughters were married. Her husband, Douglas, was in good health at age 61, and while she was staying at the Winters' house, he would be fine at home by himself.

Rosie spent most her time at the hospital, knowing the children were safe with Mrs. Galloway. The nurses had grown fond of Rosie, and their hearts went out to her and to John for the hardships they were enduring. They assumed the Winters didn't have any money, so every time they brought John's food tray, they also brought one for her. Otherwise, she would have had to do without food during her hospital visit.

It was a long two weeks, and John was eager to go home. Dr. Simpson came into his room to explain what to expect from his amputation. He approached John's bed and looked at him apprehensively. "Mr. Winters, I signed the release papers, so you can go home today. I need to explain what to expect with your stub. You see, a large percentage of amputees experience the phenomenon called phantom limbs, when folks still feel body parts that no longer exist. It may feel as though your leg and foot will ache or itch as if they're still there, but don't be alarmed. It's going to feel queer, but it's normal. Well, Mr. Winters, I wish the best to you and your family. The nurse will set an appointment for you to get your artificial leg, and then you can learn to walk again."

"I'm behholdin' to ya, Doc," John said as the doctor was leaving.

At last, he was going home. It was a cold, crisp day, two weeks before Christmas. He was incredibly happy to be able to spend Christmas at home. As Clifford turned into the driveway with John and Rosie, they could see the whole family looking out the windows, eager for his return.

As John opened the car door, Fred and Speed were waiting, wagging their tails rapidly and making whining sounds in a way that told John how much they missed him and how happy they were. He patted each head. "I missed ya, too, ol' boy."

The front door flew open and the kids came running out, shouting, "Daddy! Daddy!"

Although the family never had money for Christmas presents, the finest present they could have received was to have their daddy home for that special day. Material items were never important to the Winters. Christmas was all about family and love, and the gift of Jesus.

Each child gave John a hug and a kiss. Rosie shooed them away to give him some space, and Clifford helped him out of the car. He stood on his left leg, placed a crutch under each arm, and hobbled to the house and to his bed. He was happy to see all his children gathered around his bedside. Warm, pleasant feelings filled his heart. No amount of money could buy that. Richly blessed, and grateful just to be alive, he knew that in time he would recover.

~~ Chapter Seven ~~

The next morning as he lay in bed, John thought, *I got to concentrate on gettin' well an' gettin' usta wearin' a artificial laig. I'm tryin' not to question God about why this tragedy happen. I know it's easy to praise God when things are goin' well, but not so easy when tragedy strikes or when we're tested. But how am I suppose to take care of my family with just one laig?*

He felt Rosie turn over and gently hug him. "Good mornin'. Are ye 'bout ready for breakfus?" she asked, as she rested her head on his shoulder.

He stroked her hair. "Just lay here 'n' hug me a li'l while. You can fix breakfus in a few minutes. I really miss holdin ya like this," he said.

"Me too, darlin'. It's so good to have ya home. I missed ya so much. Try not to worry 'bout nothin' John. With the Lord's help, we'll get by somehow. I'm just so happy yer still alive an' we're still together. That's what really matters to me." she said, in a soft voice.

"I'm glad we're still together, too, honey. Tragedies like this gets a fella to thinkin' 'bout life an' the things that are really important," he said, as he softly touched her face.

"You mean everthin' to me, John." She hesitated for a moment. "There's sump'n', uh, there's sump'n' I need to tell ya." Her mouth became dry.

"What is it, honey?" He gently kissed her on the lips.

She looked at him, and her eyes widened, "John, I'm pregnant again. I musta got pregnant back in September er October," she said nervously.

With a gentle hand, he turned her face to his. "Oh, Rosie, the Lord's a-blessin' us with another bundle o' joy. I'm so happy. I love ya so much."

Joy was evident in her face. "I was so worried that you wouldn't want another young-un. We got six now, an' you've gone through so much sufferin' since yer huntin' accident."

He looked at her with unconditional love in his eyes. "Rosie, that's what life's all about, family an havin' a wonderful wife like you. Ya make me complete, for I'm nothin' without you." He paused, and chuckled, "Maybe we'll have a boy this time instead of another split-tail."

Rosie nudged him in the side with her elbow and laughed. They heard some of the kids in the next room laugh and talk as they got out of bed. Holding him close, she kissed him tenderly and whispered, "Well, I knew this huggin' wouldn't last very long. I'll get up 'n' get the fahr goin' an' start breakfus."

Half asleep, Becky walked through their bedroom on her way into the sitting room. "Mornin' Daddy, I'll help Mama fix breakfus. I'm so glad yer home for Christmas."

"I'm glad too, honey."

"Daddy, can Shane cut down a Christmas tree in the woods today? We can decorate it with some paper 'n' popcorn."

"Shore, honey. Don't pick one that's too big. Can ya bring me a glass o' water?"

"Shore, Daddy."

Becky was a kind-hearted child, always willing to help her mother. John could see that she was growing up fast. She was 14, and always tried to be responsible for the younger children. When they went to church or school, Becky always helped her mother with bathing the children and getting them dressed.

After breakfast, Shane cut down a Christmas tree. It was a spruce pine, four feet tall and Becky thought it would be perfect. The children drew Christmas bulbs on paper and colored them, to hang on the tree, with Rosie's sewing thread. And they drew pictures of stars and icicles. Becky strung popcorn and hung it around the tree. The final touch Becky added was a star, cut from a cardboard box and covered with tin foil. She placed it on the top of the tree.

"Well, how does it look?" Becky asked.

"It looks purty," Laura said.

"Yeah, the popcorn looks purty, Becky." Ellie said.

"It looks like a magic tree," Neva said, her eyes wide.

"Yeah, I think it's purty, too," Lula added.

"Yes, the tree looks good, Becky. All y'uns done a good job decoratin' it," Rosie said.

John lay in bed and listened to the wonderful sound of his family stirring about. He knew his life would be desolate without them.

~~~~~~

The day passed uneventfully. But the next morning was a school day, and as he lay in bed trying to waken, John heard Rosie call from the kitchen, "Breakfus is ready. Becky, wake up the kids. After they eat breakfus, tell 'em to get ready fer school. I don't want none o' ya'll to miss the bus."

Rosie fixed a large pan of biscuits, a huge skillet of fried potatoes, eggs and a big bowl of gravy. Sometimes, she fixed fried mackerel patties. They couldn't afford canned salmon. And they had country ham and fried apples with sugar and cinnamon. Or she fried a chicken or a couple of rabbits when John brought them home from hunting.

After breakfast, John was in the sitting room when he heard a knock at the door. "C'mon in, the door's unlocked."

Bill walked in carring a large box. He called out loudly, in a cheerful voice, "Merry Christmas. John, is it okay to set the box on the floor?"

"Shore, Bill, set it down anywhars. Can ya sit awhile?" John asked.

"Wished I could, John. I brung ya some Christmas treats from the church. We took up a collection for ya, too. Ain't much, but maybe it'll help ya out a li'l." He handed John $35.

The "treats" were brown paper bags, each of which contained an apple, orange, banana, hard candy and nuts. The gifts were from church funds to help those who didn't have money to buy gifts for their children. The children were thrilled, and John was proud to be part of a church community where folks had compassion for others.

"Thankee, Bill. Tell everybody at church we're much obliged for the money. And tell 'em to keep prayin' for us."

"I shore will, John. Everbody misses ya. Revrun Stringfield's done been preachin' since ya been away. The Lord's blessed us with some good services. We been prayin' that you'll be able to come back to church direckly," Bill said.

Rosie heard the conversation from the sitting room. As she entered, she smiled at Bill. "Do ya want some breakfus? We got plenty on the table. Just go on in the kitchen an' help yerself."

"No, thankee, Rosie, I done had my breakfus. I just come by on my way to work to wish ya'll a Merry Christmas and bring ya this box from the church."

She sat down next to John. "Merry Christmas to y'all, an' thanks for bringin' the box o' treats. Several folks from church come by to visit us since John got home from the hospital. Will ya tell everbody at church to keep prayin' for us?" she asked.

"I shore will, Rosie." Bill got up from the couch. "Well I gotta be goin'. Take care, John." he said, as he made his way out the door.

Crystal Path

The family got through Christmas, and in January nature brought a huge snowfall. They found creative ways to endure the cold months with fun recipes, and games to play. Because they couldn't afford to buy ice cream from the store, Rosie made homemade "snow cream." She gathered the snow in a large pan and added sugar, cinnamon and nutmeg - a real treat!

~~~~~

Two months had passed since John's return from the hospital, and his stub was healing nicely. He looked forward to learning how to walk when he got his artificial leg, so he could take Fred and Speed hunting again.

It was late afternoon and about time for the kids to come home from school. Rosie walked through the sitting room and sat down on the arm of John's chair. He pulled her off the chair arm, and she fell into his lap. She giggled like a little girl. Holding her gently, John gave her a kiss.

"Okay, honey, we ain't got no time for that. The kids'll be comin' home from school, an' Neva's 'bout to wake up from 'er nap." she said, with a smile on her lips.

At that moment, the kids came rushing through the front door. Becky was the first to run into the sitting room, wound-up and excited. "Guess what, Daddy? I'm gonna be in a play at school. I got lotsa practicin' to do. We're supposed to have it in April."

"That's good, Becky, you'll do just fine. One thing that makes a play good, is practice," John said.

Ellie was right behind her and out of breath. "I'm thirsty. I need a drank o' water. Mama, I got a B on my math test today."

"That's good, Ellie. You been doin' a lot better in math this year. An' you know whar the water's at, an' don't spill it all over the floor. I just mopped in thar."

Laura had a frown on her face. "I'm madder than a hornet! Today my best friends, Mary Joe 'n' Helen, was talkin' 'bout me, an' they said I'm jealous on accounta Mary Joe likes Terry Walker. He's my boyfrien'!"

"Yer too young to have a boyfriend'. An' don't worry none about Mary Joe 'n' Helen. Remember, when folks gossip an' accuse ya o' something, they're just judgin' you by their ownself."

Lula skipped into the sitting room with a smile on her face. "Mama, can I keep this? My friend Ruthie give it to me." In her right hand, she held a small blue purse with a drawstring at the top.

"Well, I don't see why not. Take good care of it, an' don't tare it up," Rosie said. She stood to go into the kitchen to start supper. Rosie was a great cook. When she prepared a meal, she didn't have to ask the kids twice to come to the table. They were always hungry.

After supper, Becky and Laura went outside to draw a bucket of water from the well, and they heated it on the stove so they could wash the dinnerware. They used two large dishpans, and Becky later threw the dishwater out the back door into the yard, while Laura dried and put the dishes away. Sometimes Rosie would throw the dirty dishwater on her plants and flowers. The soapy water also killed insects around the plants.

Darkness had come, and with the end of another day. After doing homework, it was time for the children to go to bed.

~~~~~~

The first week of March, Clifford drove John to Knoxville, 40 miles away from Coalfield, for an appointment at Sexton Prosthetic, Inc., for measurements of his leg. They had to drive into downtown, and Clifford was nervous, as he hadn't done much driving in a large city. They found the building on Broadway, and Clifford managed to park close to the building so that John wouldn't have a great distance to walk. They got out of the car, and, using his crutches, John hobbled toward the building.

Inside, they found a seat next to the door, and John leaned his crutches against an empty chair. He didn't have to wait long, when a nurse came into the room and called, "John Winters?" He raised his hand, and Clifford helped him to a standing position. "I hope this won't take long," he said.

"Don't worry about it, John, Ah hain't in no hurry."

The nurse took measurements of his stub, completed paperwork, and explained that the new leg would be ready in three weeks. She told him to wear his artificial leg only a few hours at a time. "Remember, wearin' this leg is like breakin' in a new pair o' shoes. You only wear them a few hours each day 'til they're comfortable."

Late that evening, after the day in Knoxville, John felt a heavy burden. He knew he had to call upon the Lord to find comfort for his soul. During the previous few months, it was extremely hard for him to accept the loss of his leg. He felt he was less of a man, unable to take care of his family like he once had. He had grown more depressed as each day passed. His spirit was deeply burdened with sorrow, and his cross hopelessly heavy. He had become a shadow of his former self; yet deep in his heart, he yearned to believe and trust in the Lord's goodness. He knew he shouldn't feel such emptiness, where once he felt strength and faith, but his faith seemed to grow weaker.

He wondered if the Lord had deserted him during the most tragic time of his life. Was all his hard work and praying in vain? In deep despair, John used the crutches to make his way out the back door and down the steps. A deep chill was in the air. As he slowly hobbled down the pathway leading to his altar in the woods, he felt deeply discouraged. The silent, aching pain in his soul was eating away at him. Unable to kneel, he sat on the altar and placed his crutches on the ground. He inhaled a lungful of cool air. Looking up at the sky, he prayed:

Durin' my Christian life, Lord, there's been highs 'n' lows, mountins 'n' valleys. At times, I been on top o' the mountin, touched by yer Holy Spirit. I felt like I could move that mountin, an' then Lord, I been down in the valley, an' it felt like I was all alone. Lord, each time I'm down in a valley, yer devine love gives me the strength to climb the next mountin, but, Lord, it's hard fer me to accept bein' all crippled up. I know we should never question ya, Lord, about the hardships we gotta face; but, Lord, I'm searchin' for answers why this tragedy has entered my life.

Sometimes thar's no answer but to trust ya, Lord, an' accept it. I'm weak, Lord, for I'm only a man. So I lay this burden down at yer feet. My life is in yer hands. I'm despert, Lord. My heart is breakin', an' my spirit is so low, I need your mighty hand to pick me up. I know your all-powerful an' are in control Lord. I need to feel yer sweet Holy Spirit. I pray that you'll strengthen my faith an' help me to live in the fullness of yer grace each day o' my life an' that I'll seek your will, an' not mine. I'm sorry, Lord, if I sinned against your will. Forgive me all my sins an' cleanse my soul. In Jesus holy name, I pray, Amen.

He was still for a few minutes, and then felt the spirit of God gently reach down and fill him with devine love. A rush of peacefulness swept through his soul, and he felt the weight of his burden lifted. The Holy Spirit stirred an inspiring force through his body, and he felt lighter than air. His soul soared high in a heavenly place that he never knew before. A powerful feeling of love rushed through his body as his soul danced, through the power of God. Tears streamed down his face as he lifted his eyes toward the heavens.

Using the crutches, he stood on his left foot and lifted his right hand to the sky as tears of joy rolled down his cheeks. *"Praise the Lord,"* he said. At that moment, he understood the Lord had always been with him to help through any obstacles in his life. The joy in his heart was profound and tranquil. His soul was renewed, and he had the faith he needed to serve the Lord and devote his life to Him. He realized that God never forsakes us, but it is we who stray away from Him.

Time passed slowly, and John's depression lifted. Soon it was time for Clifford to drive him to Knoxville again, to be fitted with an artificial leg. Most of the leg was made of wood. It was a bit heavy, with a hole in the bottom, an inch in diameter, to let air in, to prevent the perspiration of sweating. The nurse suggested he wear a sock over his stub so that the artificial leg wouldn't rub on the skin.

~~~~~

Occasionally, John took Fred and Speed on hunting trips not far from home. Every week, he took them into the woods and listened as they ran like powerful winds blowing with great force. Hearing them racing through the woods allowed John to imagine the feel of freedom that only legs or wings can provide.

When John hunted, he wore the artificial leg for only a short time. Even with the sock in place, his stub became extremely sore after several hours. He knew it would take some time to feel comfortable, and as time passed, he became accustomed to wearing it more often. He enjoyed being in the woods and absorbing the beauty of nature. There he could escape from everyday life. He felt at peace and close to the Lord. And he took advantage of the prayer time.

~~~~~

Early one morning in mid-April, as the sun peeked over the hill behind the house and the weather was warm, Fred and Speed lay on the grass in the backyard. All the family, except Rosie, was sleeping. She was getting ready to prepare breakfast and needed to draw a bucket of water from the well. She opened the back door and started down the steps toward the bucket and dipper kept by the back door.

She placed her foot on the first step and Fred barked at her insistently, followed by the barking of Speed. Rosie knew they were trying to warn her about something. She wondered why they carried on as they did. Speed looked under the steps and barked. Fred continued to bark, and he circled to the other side of Speed.

Rosie bent down to look, and found herself eye-to-eye with a rattlesnake. It was coiled, with its tongue darting in and out, as its rattle sounded. She realized that one more step would have placed her in a dangerous situation.

"John! Come here! Hurry! There's a snake at the back door."

John hurried out of bed using his crutches. He grabbed his shotgun from its rack, hung it over his neck and made his way to the back door. Fred and Speed had the snake surrounded. As John reached the back door, the snake began to slither away. He took aim. Bam! The shot hit the snake just below the head.

"We need to tell the young-uns to be real careful when they play outside," John said with concern. "Rattlers can strike a distance pert near two-thirds their body length an' the venom can stun or kill right away. Good thing it warnt no copperhead. When ya see one o' them, ye can bet three er four more are nearby. Copperheads always stay together, not like the rattlesnake."

He picked it up by the tail, carried it to the edge of the woods, and slung it as far as he could. He hobbled back to the house on his crutches. "Rosie, that rattlesnake had eight rattlers, one for each year. They get a new rattle ever time they shed they skin. You surprised 'im, and he felt threatened."

John looked down at Fred and Speed as they looked up at him, and he patted them. "Thanks, boys, ya'll saved Rosie's life." Speed licked his hand. Fred softly whined as if to say, *we love her too.*

"Just for that, fellas, I might give ya'll an extra biscuit for breakfus." He chuckled as he spoke.

~~ Chapter Eight ~~

After breakfast, Rosie sat at her treadle sewing machine mending the children's clothing for school. John was relaxed in his favorite chair reading the Bible, when a knock sounded at the door. "C'mon in," he called.

Joe opened the door and walked into the sitting room. He had a large brown paper bag in his hand. "I came by ta see how yer doin', John. Sorry it's taken so long ta come by."

"It's okay, I'm doin' just fine. Have a seat, Joe."

"I cain't stay away from home too long. You knowed my wife's been laid up lately." He appeared worried."

"I understand. I was thinkin' 'boutcha the other day an' wondered how you 'n' yer wife was gettin' along."

"Doin' jes fine, John. Gettin' by. I brung ya a mess o' beef. I slaughtered one o' my cows yesterdy, an' thought yer famly would like some."

"Thank ya, Joe. We shore would. Wanna cup o' coffee?"

"I reckon I would like a cup, John, if ya got some made."

"Honey, can ya put this beef into the icebox, and get Joe a cup o' coffee?"

"Shore. I'll be thar in just a minute." She answered. She stopped sewing and entered the sitting room. "Thanks for the beef, Joe. I'll put this away, in the ice box an' get yer coffee. We sure do appreciate it." She turned and walked into the kitchen, and returned with two cups of coffee.

"Here ye go, fellas. I'd best get back to my sewin'. Good to see ya, Joe. And thanks again for the beef."

Joe smiled. "Your more than welcome, Rosie,"

John took a sip of his coffee and looked at Joe, "Ya been doin' any huntin' lately?"

Joe frowned, hesitated for a moment, and nodded his head slowly. "Yup, I went hawg huntin' jes last week with Bill 'n' Lloyd Watson, he's Bill's cousin. Anyhow, Bill took his two dogs, Black, 'n' Blue. Lloyd's got two dogs, a male 'n' female, Sam 'n' Sandy. The female didn't go huntin' that day, on account she jes had a litter o' pups. Anyhow, that's the day I lost Baby Doll. I nary thought I'd miss a dawg as bad as I do 'er."

"Ya lost Baby Doll? What happen?"

Joe sighed and took a sip of his coffee, as a frown appeared on his face. "Well, we jes walked back into Catoosy about three miles, not far from whar ya got shot in the foot. Bill spotted an area whar a hawg had been rubbin' an' wallerin'. The dawgs picked up a scent 'n' lit out over a hill. We knew they was on the trail of something big. We all lit out behind the dawgs. Just when we got to the top o' that hill, we seen the dawgs down at the bottom o' the hill. They had a big ol' hawg bayed. That was the biggest hawg I ever did see. Lawdy, he had ta weigh over four hundurd pounds." He sighed and continued, "Anyhow, Bill's dawg, Blue, was facin' that ol' hawg. Lemme tell ya, he was keepin' that ol' hawg right in line an' wouldn't let him excape. He was keepin' his attention, an' the other dawgs had him surrounded. The dawgs was barkin' right in tune. That ol' hawg was hot as a fox in a forest fahr, and was screechin' like a couple o' scrappin cats. Why, I never heered the like and mad as a hornet.

An' then, as we got closer, Baby Doll come up from behind at ol' hawg, an then he swung around with his tusk an' ripped 'er side wide open. I heered 'er holler as she hit the ground. Seemed my heart fell down into my gut. I figgered my Baby Doll was too close." Joe sighed again. "It jes happen sa fast. I had my shotgun ready, an' told the dawgs ta get back so I might could get a clear shot. I took aim and fired one round an'hit 'im right between the eyes, an' he dropped like lead."

Joe glanced away from John, to avoid showing emotion, and continued, "I ran over to whar Baby Doll was alayin', an' she was barely breathin'." He paused. "John." he said in a shaky voice, "I felt such an empty feelin' inside. 'Twas hard lookin' down at 'er, an' seein' 'er like that. The cut in 'er side was 'bout ten inches long, an' she was a-bleedin' real bad. She looked up at me with 'er sad brown eyes 'n' whined, as if to say g'bye. Then she was gone. I lost my Baby Doll. John, I couldn't help it, I knelt down over her 'n' cried like a baby. I jes couldn't believe she was gone. I jes been kinda down ever since it happen."

"I hate to hear about Baby Doll, Joe. She shore was a good huntin' dawg," John said. "A fella can shore get attached to his dawgs. I'd hate it if I lost Fred er Speed. I'm a-hopin' when I get my artificial laig I can start takin' my dawgs huntin' again. The doc told me it ain't gonna be no problem larnin' to walk on my new laig. He said on accounta my laig was taken off below the knee, instead of above, it would be easier larnin' to walk. I hope he's right, cause I shore do miss huntin' with my dawgs."

"Glad ta hear that, John, I'll guess I got ta find me another good dawg. It shore will be hard to replace Baby Doll." he said as he slowly shook his head. "I might try ta get a couple o' the pups from Lloyd an' train 'em. O' course it'll take awhile to train another dawg. He said I could take my pick o' the litter. They's almost four weeks old, 'n' pert-near weaned." Joe stood up and shook John's hand. "Well John, it shore is good ta see yer gettin' along okay."

He returned the handshake. "Good to see ya, too, Joe. Now, ya come back when ya can. An' if ya see Bill, tell 'im to stop by when he gets a chaince. I'm looking forward to huntin' with you fellows again. Oh, an' thanks again for the beef."

"Will do, an' yer welcome, John. I'm a-lookin' forward ta goin' huntin' agin too. Maybe by the time I get another dawg trained, you'll be well enuff ta go. I'll be seein' ya. Take care, John."

"So long, Joe."

~~~~~

Rosie got up early the next morning to start breakfast. The house was cold, and the first thing she did was try to get the fire burning hotter. She opened the door on the potbelly stove, placed three large pieces of coal in the live ashes and left the vent door opened at the bottom of the stove for air. After getting the fire started, she walked into the kitchen to prepare breakfast.

Becky also wakened early. She was excited, as it was the day of the school play. She made her way into the sitting room and stood in her blue gown with her back close to the heating stove to warm herself. She had her hair in curlers so that it would look nice for the play.

The fire crackled in the stove, as she stood before it rehearsing her lines in the play. Suddenly, her gown caught fire. She was in a panic, not knowing what to do. She couldn't think straight, in a panic, she ran toward the kitchen, to her mother, screaming and crying. *"Help me! My back is on fahr - I'm gonna burn up, I'm gonna burn up! I'm gonna die. Mama, help me! Ahhhh!"* Running fanned the flames.

The doorways between the sitting room and John and Rosie's bedroom and between the sitting room and kitchen had thick blankets hung over each to keep the rooms warm. As Becky ran screaming into the kitchen, Rosie saw bright red flames rising behind Becky's head. She was terrified and she felt shock and nausea. She tried to grab Becky, but she turned suddenly and ran back through the doorway before Rosie could reach her. Becky ran into the sitting room, and pushed the blanket aside.

John heard the screams and leaped out of bed. He forgot about his leg, fell to the floor and landed on his stub. A knife-sharp pain shot up his leg, taking his breath away. The sound of Becky's screams caused him push the pain aside, to try to get to her.

John pulled himself up at the doorway, as the agonizing pain pierced through his leg. Becky ran close to him, as flames trailed as high as the ceiling. She was in a panic, and ran toward the front door. He knew he had to grab her before she made her way outside. John stood on his left leg, jerked down the blanket that hung in the doorway, and grabbed her as her hand grasped the doorknob. He wrapped the blanket around her, and both fell to the floor. Becky cried and screamed as John held her tightly. He pulled the blanket back to look at her face. He felt he would never forget the awful fear in her eyes.

"It's okay, Becky, the fahr's out, I gotcha, honey. Don't worry, the fahr's out" He trembled as he spoke.

Becky continued to scream, and her body shook. "My back's burnin' Daddy; my back's on fahr! My back's burnin'!" She was in a state of shock.

John asked Rosie to help get her onto the couch and onto her stomach. She placed a blanket over the couch and helped Becky lie down. John crawled to his chair and pulled himself up.

The other children were in the sitting room with wide eyes. The house smelled of burnt flesh. Becky lay on her stomach and cried in agony. And Rosie cried.

It was tremendously difficult for Rosie to accept the fact that her child was in such torment. She tried to help her lie still, but Becky continued to sob and scream - a pitiful sound that sent chills up Rosie's spine. The sound would remain with her forever.

John told Laura to get the crutches, by his bedside. He pulled himself up from the chair and quickly made his way to his bed, where he sat and put on his artificial leg. He hurried back to the sitting room. He had a sharp, throbbing pain in his leg, but he tried to block it out so that he could get help for Becky. He stopped at the front door to catch his breath. "I'll go fetch Doc Brown," he said, and he hurried out the door.

On the way to the doctor's house, John cried for his daughter. He wondered if he should've taken Becky to the hospital in Harriman. He hadn't worked since his accident, and he knew they didn't have enough money for the emergency room. If it was life-threatening I'd have no druther, *but all doctors can treat a burn. Right?*

John returned with the doctor thirty minutes later. He was a short man with a round belly, and was a bit overweight. Although he was in his early 40s, he was prematurely gray and wore round-rimmed glasses that were perched on the end of his nose.

Doctor Brown removed a pair of scissors from his medical bag and cut off the remainder of Becky's gown as she lay on her stomach. She was traumatized and trembled from the pain. The burn area started just below her shoulder blades and extended below her buttocks. Blisters as large as four centimeters in diameter had formed on her lower back. The doctor gave her a shot for pain, put some salve on the burns, and bandaged her back. He said that was all he could do then. He would return the next day.

"Please, honey, lie on yer tummy, an' try not to move around much," Rosie said, as she blinked back the tears.

Becky slept very little that night. She moaned and cried with pain until the next morning. Rosie never left her side.

The following morning, the doctor returned to check on Becky. He walked across the room and placed his medical bag on the end of the couch. He reached for his scissors to cut off the bandages. Slowly, he pulled off the bandages. Some blisters and burned skin peeled off also.

"Ahhhh!" Becky pierced the air with her screams.

Rosie scowled as she looked at the doctor. She couldn't bear to hear Becky in so much pain. As he pulled off a second bandage, John saw that the burn was deeper than he had thought, and he became concerned about infection. He commanded, "Stop, Doc. Don't pull any more bandages off. Her burns are deeper than I thought. We best take 'er to Harriman Hospital."

"That might be best. They can treat 'er better at the hospital." The doctor gathered up his supplies, placed them into his medical bag and left.

Becky was placed in the truck and rushed to the hospital.

~~~~~~

Dr. Samuel Murphy was working in ER. He examined Becky. "My word! Who has been doctoring this child? She has second and third degree burns, and some blisters have been removed. The burn areas on her back look very deep."

"Doc. Brown from Coalfield came over and treated 'er with salve 'n' bandages. Today, when he pulled the bandages off, he pulled off the blisters. I was worried 'bout infection, an' she was in a lot o' pain. I could see that the burn looked deep, so we de-cided to bring 'er here," John explained.

"Mr. Winters, that doctor doesn't know anything about a third-degree burn." Dr. Murphy asked the nurse to start an IV and give her a shot of strong antibiotic. The nurse cleaned the burn and placed her into a bed, on her stomach with a wire frame across the top, 12 inches above the mattress. The wire frame held the sheet above her, much like a tent, to keep it from touching her back.

Throughout the first week, she remained in excruciating pain. The nurses kept a close watch on her, and they treated her with pain medication through the IV. After the first two weeks in the hospital, the doctor grafted skin from the back of each leg onto her lower back.

A month had passed, and Becky remained in the hospital. Neva cried for her sister and wondered why she wasn't at home. Becky was like a second mother to Neva, and she missed her deeply. It was hard to explain to the four-year-old that her sister was in a hospital and couldn't come home. Rosie decided to take Neva to visit Becky, so she could see that her sister was okay, though Neva was too young to visit in the hospital. Rosie took Neva through a side door near the hallway that led to Becky's room. She was going to let her visit with her sister for ten minutes and then sneak her out the side door.

When Neva entered Becky's room, her eyes widened as she looked at the large sheet over Becky's back. "Becky, how come yer under that big sheet?"

"I gotta lie under this so my back can get better. They keep med'cin on my back all the time, and we cain't let the sheet touch me."

Soon, they heard a nurse coming down the hall. "Quick, Neva, stay in the privy, and be very quiet," Rosie said.

The nurse entered the room to administer pain medication. Rosie felt guilty about sneaking Neva into the hospital, so she explained the situation, and the nurse agreed to let Neva stay for ten more minutes.

When she opened the bathroom door and saw Neva, she smiled. "It's okay, honey. C'mon outta there 'n' visit with your sister. I've got an older sister, 'n' I would miss 'er terribly if she went away."

Neva was happy and excited about being allowed to stay, but she bowed her head in shyness.

"It's okay. C'mon out, Neva. You can stay an' visit for a li'l while," Rosie said, reassuring her. The nurse reached for Neva's hand. Neva hesitated, then slowly took the woman's her hand, and followed her to Becky's bed.

"I'll bet you'd like a cup o' vanilla ice-cream," the nurse suggested.

Neva nodded her head. "Yes." she whispered.

"I'll be right back with your ice-cream, an' then your mother will have to take ya on home, cuz we don't want the doctor to find ya in here. Then I'd be in trouble." She wrinkled her nose.

Neva sat quietly in a chair and enjoyed her visit. "Becky does yer back hurt real bad?"

"Not too bad, Li'l Indian, the nurses give me medcin. I'll come on home di-reckly. You'll see," Becky replied, trying to comfort her sister.

The visit was soon over, and Rosie held Neva's hand as they began to leave. Rosie paused at the door, "I'll come back tomorrah an' stay most the day, Becky."

"I love ya, Becky." Neva smiled as she spoke.

"I love ya too, Li'l Indian. Be good, 'n' I'll be home soon. Bye, Mama. See ya tomorrah."

After the visit with her sister, Neva accepted the fact that Becky would be gone a while longer.

At the end of May, Becky returned home from the hospital. Her back had healed, but she had deep, permanent scarring. The nurses had taken good care of her during her stay in the hospital. They had grown fond of Becky, and they took presents to her before she left. One was a blue gown and a blue robe to match. Another nurse gave her a pair of dark-blue house slippers. She was overjoyed to receive such wonderful things. She had never been given such beautiful gifts before. Neva and the other children were extremely happy their sister home at last.

John could finally relax, knowing his family was together again. He thanked the Lord repeatedly for sparing Becky's life.

~~ Chapter Nine ~~

The family had no money for the purchase of clothes. During the summer, Rosie made the children's clothing. Sometimes they received hand-me-downs from neighbors, or friends at church. If a family had clothing they didn't need, the items were given to the church or directly to the needy family. However, people never took money from a neighbor.

Rosie used a Singer treadle sewing machine. It had no motor; instead, it had a belt attached to the foot peddle and up to a wheel that attached to the machine. To operate it, Rosie used her feet. The faster she peddled, the faster the machine sewed. Lula had begged Rosie to make panties for her from the flour sacks she had saved, but she needed to walk down to Brooks Grocery to buy elastic.

She took Lula and Neva with her. The other children were at school. The girls walked all the way to the store, however, on the way back Neva got tired and Rosie had to carry her.

The distance to the store was more than two miles, making it difficult for Rosie in her condition. She expected her baby to be born within the following month.

Lack of money prevented her from going to a doctor during any of her pregnancies, and this one was no different. When it was time to deliver, John always had the doctor come to their home.

During the previous two weeks, John had been in a revival at Mosey Grove Church, and the revival had just ended. When John entered the room, Rosie was in the bedroom sewing.

John was enthusiastic. "Well, we had a good revival these past two weeks, an' I shore enjoyed myself. The Lord shore has blessed us in this'n. Five folks got saved, an' one of 'em was Ray Jackson. You 'member, Rosie, the daddy of the li'l girl I saved from poisonin'. Minnie's son-in-law?"

"Yes, I remember. Thank the Lord. Lotsa folks been prayin' for him for a long time. I'm so happy for Ruby. I bet she's tickled to pieces."

"Yeah, she was happy as a coon in a roastin' ear patch and was cryin' buckits. She hugged everbody in the church, an' then the whole church gathered 'round to hug Ray an' give him a friendly handshake. Ya know sump'n Rosie, when ya least expect it, the Lord sends ya a big blessin'," he said.

"I'm glad ya had a good service. I'm sorry I didn't come. I walked to the store today, an' it was hard a-walkin' back home, plus a-havin' to carry Neva part o' the way back. It's hard to move. It's a-gettin' hard to do anything."

John said jokingly, as he patting her stomach, "I don't reckon ya can get much bigger. That baby best be comin' di-reckly."

She looked at him and frowned, "If men had to have babies, they'd only be one child in each family."

He gave her a big smile, and touched her lightly on the cheek. "Yer right, Rosie, women are amazin'."

"Didja meet any new folks at the revival?"

John smiled and raised his brows. "A preacher named Arthur Crabtree who lives near Whitley City, Kentucky. I think he told me he's got 11 young-uns. He ast us to come to his home place this fall an' meet his family. He's a-wantin' me to bring my dawgs so we can go fox-huntin'. He said he's got two good foxhounds."

"When was you thinkin' about us to go to Kentucky?"

"I told 'im we'd try to get up thar in September, maybe."

"That's fine, John. Do they have room for us all? Whar's everbody gonna sleep?"

"Don't worry 'bout that none. The kids can pile up on the floor. Shucks, ya know how kids are, they can sleep anywhars."

"I'm still worried about all us a-pilin' in on a family we ain't never met before. And another thing, how's his wife gonna feed everbody?"

"I ast Arthur about that. He told me not to worry 'bout it. He said he always plants a big garden, an' they got plenty o' vittles. Besides, they only got six younguns still at home; the five oldest kids are hitched. He's a kindhearted man, Rosie. I hope you'll like him 'n' his wife."

"Well, we'll talk on it come September," she said, and continued sewing.

~~~~~~

Early on Monday morning, June 28, 1954, Rosie strained to lift herself out of bed, with a lot of back pain and cramping. She managed to cook breakfast without speaking her agony. She waited until 11 a.m. when she told John she had been having pain since 4 a.m.

His eyes widened. "Why didn't ya tell me? I best go get Doc Brown. You could have that baby anytime."

School was out for the summer, and the kids were playing outside. John called from the front door, "Laura, c'mere!"

She ran to the front door. "What, Daddy?"

"You 'n' Becky take the young-uns over to the Joneses 'n' stay. I think your mama's fixin' to have the baby. After the baby's here, I'll come 'n' gitcha. I gotta go an' get Doc Brown. Now stay over yonder 'til I come 'n' gitcha, an' tell the Joneses what's happenin'."

"Okay, Daddy." She turned and ran to tell Becky.

It took thirty minutes for John to return home with the doctor. When they walked into the bedroom, Rosie was lying in bed. With a pained expression on her face, she said, "My water just broke 'bout five minutes before ya got here. Are the kids all right?"

"They're fine. They went to the Joneses. I told 'em to stay over yonder 'til I come to get 'em. How's yer pain now?"

"I think the pains are a-comin' 'bout two to three minutes apart."

Dr. Brown set his medical bag at the foot of the bed, "Well lemme examine ya an' see how much you're dilated. We'll need some blankets to lay under ya, sump'n old we can throw away. John, I need ya to heat some water so we can clean up after the birth."

"Shore, Doc, that'll gimme sump'n to do, I'm nervous as a long-tailed cat in a room full o' rockin' chairs." His last statement brought a smile to Rosie's face.

"I already thought about the blanket an' put an' ol' quilt under me before I got into bed," Rosie said.

The doctor finished the examination. "It looks like you've dilated about five cinnymeters, Rosie, so yer about halfway thar."

"What! Only halfway? The pain is a-gettin' real bad. I cain't stand this much longer. It's worser than with my other babies. And the pain feels different. It's mostly in my back."

Dr. Brown glanced at John, and then looked at Rosie. "Well, the only thing we can do right now is to keep a-waitin' fer ya to fully dilate before ya can start pushin'."

Soon, Rosie had another sharp pain in her back. She groaned loudly. "Ohhh! My back pain is a-gettin' worser. It's a-gettin' real bad."

John noticed her hair was damp, and he watched as a bead of perspiration rolled down her cheek. At that special moment, she couldn't have been more beautiful to him. What he had given to her, she was now giving back to him, as she labored to bring forth a new life. He felt helpless as he paced the floor, worrying about his

Rosie. "Cain't ya give 'er sump'n for the pain, Doc?" John said as he paced back and forth.

"Yeah, I'll give 'er a shot of some mild pain medication. It'll help some, but I don't wanna give 'er anything very strong, on account it might hurt the baby. Lemme check ya agin, Rosie, to see how much ye done dilated. Yup, your a-gettin' closer now, Rosie. Ya dilated up to eight cinnymeters. And it appears your contractions are about one minute apart now."

She groaned with another pain, and cried out. "Ohhh! I don't think I can stand this crampin' 'n' pain in my back much longer." At a deep piercing pain, she tightly gripped the blanket beneath her. "Oh! the baby's a-comin."

Dr. Brown examined her and concurred. "I can see the head. Now, Rosie, when ya have another contraction, push real hard, as hard as ya can!"

With another sharp, cramping pain, she took a deep breath and pushed with all her strength. "Arrggh!"

"Yer doin' fine, Rosie. Yer doin' jes fine. Just rest a minute, an' when ya feel another pain, push as hard as ya can."

Another surge of pain shot from her stomach to her back and up her spine. As she pushed with all her might, she felt the baby leave her body. Instantly, she heard a beautiful sound, as the baby cried. Her heart beat faster, as blissful joy filled her soul. She cried tears of happiness.

"It's a girl, Rosie, a be-utiful baby girl," Dr. Brown announced.

"She is be-utiful, Rosie. I'm so glad yer pain is finally over," John said.

Ten minutes passed while the doctor cleaned up the baby, and listened to her breathing and monitored her heart rate.

"Oh! I'm havin' another pain," Rosie cried out.

Dr. Brown checked her. "Here comes another'n. Rosie, yer havin' twins. The next time ye got pain, push as hard as ya can!"

"Twins! I cain't believe it! We're havin' twins! Well ain't that sump'n? Thankee Lord." John said, with a smile from ear to ear.

Soon, Rosie felt another hard contraction. "Push, Rosie, the doctor said. Push as hard as you can. Give it all ye got. Push!" She bore done hard and gasped for air.

"I'm a little excited, the doctor said. These are the first twins I've delivered. Your doin' fine Rosie. I can see the head."

Rosie was groaning and pushing when she felt the head slip out, with less pain than the last. She rested for a moment, and felt another contraction. She took a huge breath, began to bear down again, and tightly grasped the quilt under her. With an intense, tearing pain, she brought forth her last baby. Rosie was relieved it was over; the pain and suffering were worth it.

The second baby began to cry. "It's a boy, Rosie, ya got a baby boy," the doctor said.

Rosie's heart filled with joy. She laughed and cried simultaneously. Her hair was plastered to her face, as she looked up at John. With her strength completely drained, she was too weak to lift her head off the pillow.

John was thrilled. He desperately wanted another son. He grabbed Dr. Brown in a bear hug, lifted him off the floor and swung him around.

The doctor's face became crimson. He was surprised and embarrassed. "Well, John, yer about the happiest fella I've seen in a long time." The doctor laughed.

John smiled broadly. "I gotta go over to the Joneses an' tell the young-uns about this. Twins! Wow, this here's gonna be a big suprise. I'll be back in a few minutes, Rosie, I love ya!" He rushed out the door feeling on top of the world. At that moment, everything was perfect. He pulled onto the road leading to Clifford's house. As he approached, he saw the kids in the front yard playing tag. He sounded the horn, and when he stopped the truck the kids ran up and all were talking at the same time.

"Did Mama have the baby, Daddy?" Becky asked excitedly.

"Is Mama okay, Daddy?" Laura asked.

"Daddy, did the doctor bring us a new baby?" Lula asked.

Ellie ran up behind Lula. "Is it a girl er boy?"

"Have I gotta brother or sister?" Shane asked, hoping for a little brother.

John strutted like a rooster. "It's a girl and a boy. Yer mother had twins. Climb into the truck, kids, an' we'll go on home an' see Mama an' yer new brother 'n' sister."

Daisy heard the commotion outside, and she stepped onto the porch. "Did she have the baby? Be it a girl er boy?"

They all called at the same time, *"Both!"*

"Thankee, Daisy, for watchin' the young-uns."

"Glad ta do it, John. I'll come up 'n' see Rosie and the babies in a day er two."

Upon their return home, they found Rosie and the twins lying in bed. She had a joyful expression, with a baby lying on each arm. A soft glow surrounded her face as she looked adoringly upon her newborn babies. She was a proud mother. The pain and suffering now forgotten, all her kids were worth it.

She looked up at her children. "Come see yer new sister an' brother. I decided to name the girl Janie Lynn an' the boy Jamie Lee." Everyone was excited and spoke simultaneously..

Dr. Brown interrupted. "John, can ya have the children step out for just a few minutes? Sump'n I need to talk to you 'n' Rosie about."

John motioned with his hand for the kids to leave the room. "You young-uns go into the sittin' room for awhile." John turned to the doctor with concerned. "What is it, Doc?"

"I feel thar's a problem with the girl. Her breathin' an' heartbeat hain't a steady rhythm the way they oughta be. Maybe ya oughta take both to Harriman Hospital an' get 'em checked. The boy appears fine, but get him checked when ya take the li'l girl." He picked up his medical bag and walked to the door. He turned to look at Rosie. "Now, Rosie, ya take good care o' yerself an' them babies an' lemme know if ya need me for anything."

"I will, an' thankee, Doc. I'll go right back to bed after the hospital trip." *She learned from her grandmother and great-grandmother that after a woman delivered a baby, she was to stay in bed for nine days. They believed that was the length of time it took for the womb to go back into place.*

As soon as the doctor left, the kids rushed back into the bedroom to get another look at the twins. John didn't miss the worry on Rosie's face.

She looked up at him and spoke. "We oughta try an' take the twins to the hospital tomorrah, to see if anything's wrong."

"Okay, we'll go first thing in the mornin'. Shane 'n' Becky can watch the kids 'til we get back."

"Is sump'n wrong with the babies, Mama?" Becky asked. She reached to touch Janie's head.

"I don't think so, Becky. Doc Brown wants the hospital doctor to look 'em over. We'll take 'em tomorrah. I'm shore they'll be fine."

~~~~~

Upon arrival at the hospital early the next morning, John found a wheelchair inside the entrance for Rosie. He helped her into the chair, and Rosie held a baby in each arm. He pushed her, along with the babies, to the examining room. They saw Dr. Simpson in the emergency room. The doctor recognized John and smiled. "Reverend Winters, I see you've brought two little bundles."

"Doctor Simpson, my wife jes had the twins yesterday, an' Doc Brown said the girl wasn't breathin' right."

"Well, let's put them on the table and have a look-see." He motioned for the nurse to come into the room. "Can you measure and weigh these babies, please?"

"Yes, Dr. Simpson, I shore will. This'll only take a few minutes," she said as she took one baby from Rosie's arms.

Crystal Path

"John, do ya reckon sump'ns wrong with Janie?" Rosie asked, with a frightened look in her eyes.

"Now, honey, don'tcha worry. The doctor'll take good care of 'em here at the hospital."

"I don't know if I can go through losin' another baby, John. That's one thing that just breaks yer heart, an' never stops tarin' atcha from the inside. Sometimes, I cain't help but think of our first two babies we lost, an' wonderin' what they woulda looked like if they lived."

"Now, honey, don'tcha go thinkin' like that. Yer upset right now, an' ya done been through a lot o' pain havin' these babies. They're gonna be all right. The Lord is watchin' over 'em," he said.

"You're right, John, they'll be all right. They have to."

The nurse brought the babies back into the room. "The boy is 19 inches long an' weighs seven an a half pounds; the girl is 18½ inches long an' weighs seven pounds. These are big babies for twins, Mrs. Winters."

"Yes, I know; I felt big as a barrel, an' it was hard to move." Rosie grinned. "When they start a-comin two at a time, it's time to quit."

The nurse laughed. "That seems reasonable to me."

Twenty minutes later, Dr. Simpson entered the room sighed. "Mr. and Mrs. Winters, I feel it would be best to keep both babies and place them into an incubator. The boy should stay two days, just for precaution, but the little girl will need to stay longer. Her breathing is not steady, the way it should be."

Rosie looked at her twins with tears in her eyes. "If that's what's best for the babies. Will they be all right?"

"They should be fine, Mrs. Winters. We just need to make sure their lungs are strong and everything's working properly before they go home. We'll fix you a bed in the room next to the nursery."

After the doctor left the room, Rosie closed her eyes and sent a silent plea to heaven. *Lord, please let the twins be all right. Don't take one of the babies from us, Lord; please, not now. Let 'em both live.* She raised her head to look at John. He was praying, too. When he opened his eyes, he gave her a warm smile.

The days passed slowly as Rosie spent most of her nine-day bed rest at the hospital. Jamie stayed three days, and Janie eight days before they were able to go home.

In mid-August, John received a letter from Kentucky. The name on the return address was *Arthur Crabtree:*

Dear John and famly,

Hope yer famly doin' fine. We want to invite you ta come up an' do some fox-huntin'. My wife is wanted to meet your famly. We're hopin' you'all can come up on a Friday and stay all weekend with us. Your more than welcome to come up in September, and we want you'all to feel right at home. Write back and let me know when un's can come. Hope to see ya soon.

Arthur and famly

After receiving the letter, John began preparing for the trip to Kentucky.

~~ Chapter Ten ~~

On a Friday afternoon in September, when the weather had turned cooler, the Winters family left for Kentucky to meet the Crabtree family. Their plans were to stay until Sunday evening. Rosie was in the front seat with one twin, and Becky sat in the middle with the other baby. In the back of the truck, on each side, were long benches. Fred and Speed lay in back next to the double panel doors.

The distance from Coalfield to Whitley City was 80 miles, making total driving time about two hours. Highway 27 was a two-lane winding road. Every three or four weeks, a bulldozer graded all the backcountry gravel roads.

Ann Eva Graves

John had been driving for about an hour when they passed the town of Oneida and were close to the Kentucky state line. The kids were hungry, and they began to snack on homemade cookies.

"Lula has more cookies than I do," Laura complained.

"So what! I got two cookies. You can get more."

"Yer just greedy, Lula."

"Mama, Laura said I was greedy."

"Laura, no more name callin'. Lula, just let it go in one ear 'n' out the other. Everbody share the cookies. An' ya best settle down. I don't wanna hear any more fussin'." There was firmness in Rosie voice.

Neva sat on the bench next to Lula and moaned, as if something were hurting her.

"Li'l Indian, what's the matter with ya?" Rosie asked. Neva didn't hear her mother above the noise in the back of the truck, and she continued to groan.

Rosie turned her head. "What's the matter, Neva? What do you want?"

"My belly hurts, that's what I want!"

Rosie and John looked at each other and tried to keep from laughing. "Okay, Li'l Indian, sit still. It's not much further; an' we'll be at the Crabtree's."

"How much further, Daddy?" Becky asked.

"Not much 'bout ten er fifteen minutes. Hey, kids, we're in Kentucky. We just crossed the state line." John and Rosie enjoyed the scenery as they drove by several farms with large barns and cattle grazing in the fields. "Hey, kids, look here at all the purty scenery. This state has miles of streams, an' it has the biggest artificial lake east o' the Mississippi. And, it's the only state that's got rivers on three sides - the Mississippi, Big Sandy and the Ohio River to the north. They re-stocked a lot o' wildlife in this state an' a lot a foxes 'n' wild turkey. They oughta have some good huntin' up here."

As they drew closer, the children became increasingly more excited about their arrival at the Crabtree's house. They were near Whitley City, and John knew they would arrive soon. After rounding a curve, he saw the name Crabtree on a mailbox, and he announced loudly, "We're finally here, kids."

The house sat sixty yards from the highway. As they drove up into the driveway, they saw a large white house with four steps leading up to a huge porch across the front and white-framed windows with black shutters. Shrubbery was in front of the porch, and a tire swing hung from a big oak tree. The house had a large stone chimney from which smoke drifted.

When the Crabtree family heard the truck, Arthur and his wife Millie came onto the front porch to give them a warm welcome, followed by their kids.

Arthur walked down the steps and called out a greeting. "Glad to see ya, John. Tell yer kinfolks to get out an' c'mon in."

John slowly got out, and opened the double doors behind the truck to release his dogs. He had them tied with rope and he led them up to the porch. They barked their hellos and wagged their tails, and the kids climbed out of the truck.

Arthur stood at the bottom of the steps and shook John's hand. "Real glad yer here, John. Now, you 'n' yer famly make yerselves right at home. I got a place fer yer dawgs around back whar my two dawgs, Bo 'n'

Rocky, are. I been looking forward to our huntin' trip." Arthur and John headed to the backyard.

Millie approached Rosie, with a smile. "Arthur said yer name's Rosie. I'm Millie. Glad to have ya. Ever since Arthur came back from the revival in Tennessee, he been talkin' 'bout how he enjoyed hearin' John preach. It appears they become good friends. Arthur's been a-lookin forward to huntin' with John."

Rosie knew immediately that she was going to like Millie, who had kindness in her voice and compassion in her eyes. She was surprised that Millie didn't look old enough to have 11 children. Rosie had been told her age was 45. She was short, and Rosie guessed her height at 5' 2" and weight at 150 pounds. She had a round, smooth face and salt and pepper hair. She had a young and vibrant appearance.

Millie walked up the steps of the porch, looked at her children, and began to introduce them, "These here is our young-uns, we got six at home, an' five that are married 'n' gone. This is Jack. He's 16. Amy, she's 14. An' this here's Mandy. She's 11. Mary's seven; Tommy's five; an' Susan's three. She's my baby."

Rosie proudly introduced her clan, "This is my oldest, Shane. He's 15. Becky, she's 14; Laura's ten; Ellie, she's nine; Lula's six; Neva's three. We sometimes call her Li'l Indian; an' the twins, Janie 'n' Jamie, are three months old."

"I reckon ya got a lot o' extry work, takin' care o' twins."

"Yeah. I always heard twins are double trouble. I told John, when they start a-comin' two at a time, it's time to quit!" Both woman laughed.

"After the 11th child, I was beginnin' to wonder when they was gonna stop a-comin', too." Millie tried to adjust the blue and white apron tied around her waist. "C'mon in, Rosie. You can keep me comp'ny while I start supper. All ya kids stay in the yard 'n' play." She motioned with her hand for Rosie to follow her.

"You cain't do all the cookin' for this bunch by yerself. Just tell me whatcha want me to do, an' I'll help."

"Rosie, y'uns are gonna stay all weekend with us, ain'tcha? Me 'n' Arthur want ya'll to feel right to home. I got Susan's baby bed outta the attic, cleaned it up, an' put it out fer the twins, so they'll have a bed while yer here."

"That's right kind of ya to fix the twins a bed. I'll lay 'em down 'n' help ya with supper." She followed Millie into the kitchen. Glancing out the window, she saw John and Arthur with the dogs. They were chatting, with big grins, and no doubt talking about hunting.

While preparing supper, the two women became fast friends. Each exchanged information about their children and the grades they received in school.

And they exchanged stories about how they had met their respective spouses. Rosie related:

"My dad 'n' John liked fox-huntin together. I had feelin's for 'im, but I thought he liked one of my older sisters. I got two. Well, anyhow, one day I was arunnin' through the house to go out the back door to tell my daddy something. John was a-standin' in the kitchen when I come through the doorway. He grabbed me, pull me into his arms, an then kissed me tender-like. I was so happy, my heart just melted at that moment, for I felt a special feelin', an' I knew I was in love. It was as if our hearts touched and his sweet love filled my soul. I forgot what I was a-runnin' out the back door to tell my dad. Then he got to courtin' me, an' it din't take long to

know he was the one to make my life complete, an' the one I was aimin to spend the rest of my life with."

Millie smiled as Rosie told her story, and she told Rosie how she met Arthur:

"We went to the same church. I was 17 an' he was 20. He kept watchin' me 'n' grinnin' at me. O' course, I smiled back at 'im. He ast me if I wanted to go on a picnic down by the pond neah his house. His famly dint live a fer piece from the church on acounta his paw was pastor of the church. The way he looked at me, an' the way he talked to me, well, on that picnic, I knew I was a-fallin' in love with 'im. He touched my heart, an' I knew I would nary be able to walk away from 'im, an' he was the one fer me. And now we been married fer pertnear 27 years."

When dinner was ready, Millie called for everybody to gather around the table. One announcement worked for all the kids. They were hungry, after hard play. Millie and Rosie had prepared more than enough food for both families, with no room to set out another dish. A long bench behind the oak table seated the children. On the wall behind the table was a large picture of *The Last Supper.*

Millie had prepared a large platter of fried chicken, mashed potatoes, green beans she had canned from her garden and fresh corn on the cob, also from the garden. She baked a large pan of corn bread, two loaves of sweet-smelling, homemade bread, sliced tomatoes, coleslaw and macaroni and cheese. For desert, melt-in-your- mouth peach cobbler and a large chocolate cake.

As the families' gathered around the table, Millie motioned for everyone to bow their heads, and Arthur said grace:

"As we gather 'round the table, Lord, we ast ya to bless these food fer the nourishment of our bodies. We thankee, Lord fer yer love, fer this special day, an' the way our famlys have come together in frien'ship. Look down on us, an' bless this day, Lord. In Jesus' name we pray. Amen."

When the meal was over and the dishes were washed and put away, everybody went to the front porch to sit, relax and talk. Arthur was talented at playing a guitar, and he could make a banjo sing a pretty tune. His son Jack could play a guitar extremely well, and also a harmonica. Arthur and Jack played several hymns. Arthur changed to a different style of music, and picked *'Will You Be My Sweetheart'?*

Millie and Rosie sang the tune. John said, "I'm already yer sweetheart," and he winked at Rosie. They stopped singing and laughed.

Arthur finished the song and grinned. "Well, that's enuff music. I bes' put this banjo 'n' guitar up fer the night."

Millie and Rosie remained on the porch visiting, while the kids played in the front yard, until just before dark, when they tried to get everyone settled in bed. And John and Arthur continued their talk about dogs and their big hunting trip planned for early the next morning.

The men got up at 4 a.m. on Saturday. They got their shotguns and loaded the dogs into the back of Arthur's truck. When they arrived at the hunting area, Arthur parked the truck. They got their guns and dogs and walked into the wooded area.

"It ought to not take long fer the dawgs to pick up a scent. Thar's plenty o' foxes in this area. I been huntin' here for years," Arthur said.

They had walked 60 yards, when the dogs started to bark. They were 30 yards ahead and began to run like lightning toward a hill. Soon they were out of sight. John listened for a time "That's Fred's bark," he said. "He's picked up a scent."

"Yup, they got 'im on the run. They're right on 'im an' it sounds like they closin' in. I can hear my dawg, Bo. He won't let that fox get away. Shucks, Bo'll, run that fox all day if he has to. The dawgs are stayin' right together. Shore is purty music to yer ear, hain't it, John?"

John cupped his hand over his ear to listen. "Yeah, Arthur, I enjoy hearin' my dawgs bark. Fred got the most sweet-soundin' bark. Sometimes I wonder if he ain't tryin to sing to that ol' fox. I don't wanna lose the dawgs," John said, as he walked faster toward the noise. "It's hard to keep up. I cain't walk as fast as I usta, since I lost my laig."

Arthur turned his head in the direction of the dogs. "Don'tcha worry, John, they'll give that ol' fox a good run."

They could hear the dogs just beyond the next hill, and they clearly were running farther from them.

They had walked for several hours when John spoke. "I can barely hear 'em now. The fox led 'em over yonder tord that ridge." He walked to a log that lay on the ground and sat down. "I gotta rest here awhile. My leg is gettin' a might sore."

"Shore, John, we can rest a spell. Even if we lose em, my dawgs know the way back to the house."

"Sorry to slow ye down. I got a hitch in my gitalong these days. Wearin' this artificial laig gets mighty sore after a few hours. I reckon' I oughta quit complainin' an' just be grateful I can walk at all."

Arthur, too, was tired. "We'll rest a few minutes."

The sun shone through the treetops in early afternoon, as they sat in the woods. It was calm and peaceful, except for the singing of a bird. The air smelled clean and fresh, and it was good to sit and enjoy the quietness.

"It feels nice to just sit calmly an' soak in the beauty of God's creation," John said. He inhaled deeply.

"A higher power had to create such a glorious earth," Arthur said.

When they could no longer hear the dogs, they stood up and walked in the direction in which they had last heard them. They made their way to the ridge, and using his fox-horn, John called for the dogs, then listened. But they heard no barking. Arthur called his dogs, but no response.

Arthur said. "I knowed they come in this direction," "Ain't no telling how far that fox'll run 'em. No need to worry, John, my dawgs done been huntin' in these woods a long time. It'll be dark in a few hours, an' they oughta be a-comin' back this-a-way di-reckly. If we cain't find 'em tonight, they'll be at the house by mornin'." Arthur called again. No response.

Both men knew the hunting instinct is so strong, that when a foxhound detects a scent it will follow it, sometimes ignoring commands. It can run hard for hours. And for hours they waited, until the sun was behind the distant hill.

"John, do ye reckon we oughta get back to the house? My dawgs'll lead yer dawgs back by mornin'. No tellin how far they'll run that fox."

John appeared worried. "I reckon yer right, we oughta get back, but I shore hate leavin' 'em out here. If they ain't at yer house by daylight, we got to come back out here tomorrah 'n' look for 'em again. If they're nearby an' hear me callin', they generly come right away."

Darkness settled around the men when they returned to the truck. John called his dogs again. Still no response. It was 7 p.m., as they began the drive toward Arthur's home.

When they arrived back at Arthur's house, they immediately went to bed. John didn't rest well. He slept for three hours, and wakened at 5 a.m. on Sunday. He got out of bed, put on his clothes, and walked outside to the front porch, to see if any of the dogs had returned.

The morning sky was a deep golden hue as the sun peeked over the hill in front of Arthur's house. The morning air was cool and crisp. The dogs had not returned. John was greatly concerned. He didn't want to leave without his dogs.

Arthur came out on the front porch and sat in a chair next to John. "Well, I don't know what to think, John. When I got separated from my dawgs onest before, they come back on home the next mornin' before daylight."

John frowned and rubbed his chin. "Do ya reckon maybe somebody got 'em, er maybe they're dead?"

"Don'tcha go thinkin' that-a-way, John. They'll come back di-reckly. You'll see." Arthur tried to reassure him.

"Your right, I trained them well. They should be comin' back by mornin'." John said.

Daylight had just broken when they heard Millie call out from the kitchen, "Breakfus is ready. Come 'n' eat. You two fox-hunters get in here 'n' eat breakfus."

Most of the family was seated at the table except for the three youngest children, who were still asleep. Millie noticed the worried expressions on the men's faces. "Yer dawgs hain't come back yet? Now don'tcha worry, Arthur. They'll be back later today, jes like before."

After breakfast, Arthur reached for his Bible. "Let's get ready 'n' go to Sundy school. I done told everbody at church 'bout our friends, an' I wanna hear Rosie sing. Let's get on over to the church an' have a good ol'-fashioned meetin'. The dawgs ought to be here when we get back."

"Yeah," John said. "Let's everbody go to church. I hope the dawgs come back before church services are over. I don't believe in huntin' on Sundy, so if they ain't back by late evenun, we got to head on back to Tennessee. I gotta go to work Mondy mornin'. I'd shore hate to go home without my dawgs."

~~~~~~

The congregation gave the Winters family a warm welcome. Rosie sang a couple of songs, and they enjoyed her singing. Arthur invited John to preach and suggested he let the Lord guide him with His Holy Spirit. John stood and walked behind the pulpit, opened his Bible and began to speak.

"First, I wanna thank the Lord for savin' my soul, an' thank Him that I'm able to be here today. I enjoyed the service thus far. Pray for me while I try to de-liver the Word o' God. Today, the Holy Spirit would like me to preach about *'Why do we need a Savior'?"*

If you'd like to foller along, please open yer Bible to John, Chapter 3, startin' with verse one through seven. And then, verses 15 through 18." He read aloud:

> *There was a man of the Pharisees, named Nicodemus, a ruler of the Jews:*
>
> *The same came to Jesus by night, and said unto him, Rabbi, we know that thou art a teacher come from God: for no man can do these miracles that thou doest, except God be with him.*
>
> *Jesus answered and said unto him, Verily, verily, I say unto thee, Except a man be born again, he cannot see the kingdom of God.*
>
> *Nicodemus saith unto him, How can a man be born when he is old? Can he enter the second time into his mother's womb, and be born?*
>
> *Jesus answered, Verily, verily, I say unto thee, Except a man is born of water and of the Spirit, he cannot enter into the kingdom of God.*
>
> *That which is born of the flesh is flesh; and that which is born of the Spirit is spirit.*
>
> *Marvel not that I said unto thee, Ye must be born again.*

After reading the Bible verses, John said, "Now go on down to verses 15 through 18." He cleared his throat and continued to read:

> *That whosoever believeth in him should not perish, but have eternal life.*

For God so loved the world that he gave his only begotten Son, that whosoever believeth in him should not perish, but have everlasting life.

For God sent not his Son into the world to condemn the world; but that the world through him might be saved.

He that believeth on him is not condemned: but he that believeth not is condemned already, because he hath not believed in the name of the only begotten Son of God.

John paused. "Now, I know there are many religions in this world an' a fella is free to believe what he wants to. That's why God give us freedom o' choice. However, my Bible tells me that a man cannot enter the Kingdom of God on his good looks, or buy his way in, nor work his way there. Jesus said you must be born again."

The church was quiet, as John continued. "There's a natural birth an' a spiritual birth. I cain't tell ya much about my first birth comin' into this sinful world, but the second birth, through the Holy Spirit, now that's sump'n I love to talk about.

I believe in eternal salvation. Please don't get me wrong. I'm not sayin' that after you're saved you can just live anyway you want too. After a man accepts the Lord as his personal Savior, it's necessary to live for the Lord, to keep the joy of yer salvation. God don't force us to live for Him. The reason a Christian ought to live fer the Lord is to show the world that yer a Christian.

My Bible leads me to believe that onest yer saved, yer always saved. Some folks believe if ya backslide, then ya have to get saved a second time. Let me tell ya, brother, when God saves yer soul, he does the job right the first time. Onest you're born into the family o' God, there ain't nobody can undo that birth. It's the same way with my family. Each time a baby is borned, that birth cain't be undone. There is a natural birth and a spiritual birth.

After Adam 'n' Eve sinned in the garden, an' sin come into the world, then every child that is born into this world is born into sin. God knew man couldn't find a way into His Kingdom on his own efforts; that's why a Savior was sent. Jesus paid our sin debt on Calvary, when He died for our sins. I ast ya again, *Why do we need a Savior?"*

If ya backslide, all ye need to do is repent. The Bible says to repent daily, for all of us sin an' come short o' the glory o' God, each day of our lives. Some folks believe that adultery and drinking moonshine whiskey is the only sins there are. But let me tell ya, brother, to have a evil thought is a sin, and backbiting, jealousy, haterd, greed, the pride of life, lying, murder, stealin' and failin' to pray or read yer Bible is a sin, and that's just a few. As sinful as the human race is, I don't understand how anybody can believe that he or she can go to heaven on their good works. We don't have a thing to do with salvation. *Only by Grace, we are saved.*

I've heard some folks say that lying will send ya to hell. Folks, the only thing that condemns ya is not excepting Jesus as yer personal Savior. If there was any other way for us to enter God's kingdom, any other way at all without Jesus, then Jesus comin' into this world was in vain. Jesus is the only way, for there is no other way.

God give the world the gift of His only begotten Son, an' it's up to you to accept that gift. Folks Jesus is comin back someday; are you ready? You got the freedom to choose where ya aim to spend eternity. It's simple. Just open up yer heart an' let the Savior in. Believe from deep within yer heart. That's the way to got saved. It's that simple."

John closed his Bible and looked at the congregation. "Would ever'body stand an' sing an invitation song? The altar is open to anybody who would like to accept the Lord as their personal Savior or come to pray if yer heart is burdened.

Before I turn the services back over to brother Crabtree, I wanna thank the Lord for His many blessin's. I need yer prayers that the Lord will lead an' guide me each day o' my life an' pray that He would strengthen my faith that I would grow stronger in the Lord. Revrun Crabtree, I turn the services back over to you. May the Good Lord bless y'all. An' please keep my family in yer prayers." John felt he had followed the Holy Spirit. Everyone clearly enjoyed the sermon.

Arthur stood and shook John's hand. "Good preachin'. I enjoyed that very much." He motioned with his hand for everyone to stand and sing. Softly, they began to sing *'What a Friend We Have in Jesus'*.

~~~~~~

That afternoon, they went back to the wooded area where they lost the dogs. John got out of the truck and called his dogs with his fox-horn, but had no response. Usually, when the dogs heard the fox-horn, they would quickly return. The fox-horn was part of their training.

"Let's walk over to that hill whar we heered 'em last night. If my dawgs are in the area an' hear me callin', they'll come. I trained my dogs in these woods." Arthur said.

"Yup, my dawgs oughta come back to me when they hear me callin'. That's why it's hard to figah out what happen to 'em last night. I got to leave in a few hours, an' I hate leavin' my dawgs," John added.

As they walked across an open field, Arthur said, "Now, John, don't worry none. If the dawgs come back, I'll take good care of 'em. I'll bring 'em on down to yer house. If all the dawgs are still together, they'll come back home sooner er later."

"If they come back, you can call Brooks Grocery Store in Coalfield, an' they'll lemme know. Then I'll come up here 'n' get 'em."

"Yes, John, I'll call Brooks Grocery when they come back." They called the dogs one last time, but didn't hear them barking. They decided to return to Arthur's house.

It was getting late. John held out his hand for a handshake. "Arthur, I'd best get back on home. I want to thankee fer everthin', an' making us feel welcome. I shore enjoyed spending time with yer family, an' hope ya can come to Tennessee 'n' visit us soon."

"I'm feelin' real bad 'bout yer dawgs, John. If I find 'em, I'll shore take good care of 'em."

"I knowed ya will. Don'tcha feel bad about this. They just got away from us. Maybe they'll come back to yer house in a day er two. I'll be seein' ya, Arthur. You an' yer famly's welcome to come visit us if ever you feel like it."

"So long, John."

John loaded his family into the truck and started home. As bad as he needed money, he wouldn't have sold his dogs for any amount. Several hunters in Tennessee offered to buy the dogs from him, but he wouldn't part with them. He was terribly upset, knowing he had to return home without them. He couldn't believe he had lost them. He wondered if they were in an accident, and if they were dead. It was a long and worrisome drive to Coalfield. All he could do was pray that they were safe and that they would be returned to him soon.

~~ Chapter Eleven ~~

The Winters family arrived home late on Sunday evening. The lack of fire in the heating stove made the house cold. John started a fire with paper, small pieces of kindling and pine. Gradually, the house became warm. The kids were glad to be at home. They were exhausted.

With thoughts of his dogs, John had difficulty sleeping. He knew he had trained them well, and they should make their way back to Arthur's house soon. He prayed that Arthur would get his dogs back also. He would have to wait for Arthur to leave a message at the grocery store. He could make another trip to Kentucky, but that would have to wait a while, for lack of money.

He was inconsolable, and had a difficult time accepting the fact that his dogs were gone. He tossed and turned all night. He eventually got three hours of sleep and wakened at 5 o'clock. He had to go to work. After the hunting accident, he worked part time.

The dogs had provided him with great enjoyment. He loved to listen to them bark when they were on a fox-hunt. He had many fond memories of hunting with them. They seemed to enjoy the hunt as much as he did. They were the best fox-hunting dogs he had ever owned, and he knew he would never find foxhounds that could replace them. Several hunters in the community were amazed by the dogs' talents and hunting skills.

~~~~~~

Arthur got up early Monday morning and opened the back door. To his surprise, Bo and Rocky came to the back porch to greet him. They had numerous scrapes on their bodies, and they clearly were exhausted and hungry. Arthur looked around the yard for John's dogs, but didn't see them. He called for them, but no response.

He gave his dogs food and water, and walked to the front of the house and called out again to John's dogs. He called again, but John's dogs were nowhere around.

Arthur went back to look at his dogs again. When they had finished eating, he rubbed Bo on his head. "Boy, if ya could only talk 'n' tell me what happen to John's dawgs." He wondered why they didn't stay together. Could someone have captured John's dawgs?

He decided he would travel around in his community and ask everyone if they had seen two foxhounds. The town was small and everyone knew everyone else. He hoped someone could give him some good news.

After the fox hunt, the dogs returned on Sunday morning to the area where Arthur had parked the truck. With no truck and no Arthur or John, Bo and Rocky began the trek toward home. Fred and Speed remained behind. Arthur's dogs barked for them to follow, but they wanted to wait for their master. A couple of hours later, when they realized John was not in the area, they decided to go home. *Their home.*

~~~~~

They hadn't eaten for two days, and were hungry and thirsty. Fred started barking. He could smell water. Speed smelled it too. Panting, they ran down a path that led to a stream. Sunlight streamed through the treetops and was reflected on the water. After drinking their fill, Speed started downstream. Speed's sense of direction led them south, toward the mountains.

The dogs were 10 miles from Arthur's house when they ran out of the woods and came upon an open field. In search of food, they headed toward a nearby house.

A man was inside listening to the radio. William Johnson loved listening to bluegrass banjo-picking music. He lived by himself, since his wife death, and his house was a cluttered mess. Inside a shed behind his house was a still for making whiskey. He spent most of his time sitting in a chair drinking moonshine and smoking Prince Albert tobacco. He was sixty years old, a bit heavy, and going bald. The man always bore a frown, with a miserable look on his face and anger in his eyes. He felt sorry for himself, a cantankerous old man.

It was late in the afternoon and the air was cool and crisp. Fred and Speed were 20 yards from the house. They could hear the radio blaring. William stood up from his chair and staggered into the kitchen to get another jug of whiskey. He glanced out the window and saw the dogs as they were coming around the shed. He grabbed his rifle and threw the back door open.

"So, you two are the ones that's been killin' my chickens. I'll gitcha onest an' fer all, ye damn dawgs." He raised the rifle and fired at Speed, missing him by inches. Both dogs began running toward the woods. William fired another shot and hit the ground a foot short. The dogs reached the woods just before William fired a third shot.

At last, deep into the woods, they were safe from gunfire. They slowed their pace. They were tired and hungry. They came upon a stream running smoothly over rocks, and they drank their fill of water. A bed of grass near an oak tree looked inviting. Exhausted, as they were, food would have to wait. They lay down close together and immediately fell asleep. *They dreamed of reuniting with John and the rest of the family.*

Daylight was shining through the leaves of the trees. They instinctively knew that dawn was breaking and that rest time was over. Speed made his way to the stream for water, followed by Fred. They instinctively knew they should head toward the mountains. If they had been in East Tennessee, in familiar territory, they would have had more insight in how to find their way home. In fact, they were two miles east of Pine Knot, Kentucky, not far from the Tennessee state line.

Just over the next hill was the Scott family. Cathy and Tim Scott had a four-room house made of rough lumber that Tim had built. He painted the outside boards with crude oil to keep them from decaying.

Tim was 31 years old with a firm, handsome face. He was tall and thin with black hair and brown eyes. Cathy was one year older, with the same eyes and hair. Her hair hung halfway down her back. Clay, ten years old, was a skinny boy, small for his age, with dark brown hair and brown eyes, like his mother and daddy. Amy was a sweet seven-year old, who resembled her mother. Tim had a good rabbit-dog, a fine-looking beagle named Sniffles. He was black and tan, with white on his face and belly.

"Clay will ya take the table scraps out 'n' feed the dawg?" Tim asked, when the family had finished breakfast.

"Shore, Paw. Then kin we go huntin'? Mebe we might could kill us a rabbit fer supper. Nobody cooks a rabbit like Maw."

"Son, I promised I'd take ya tomorrah."

"I still think he's too young to start huntin'. He oughta to wait a couple 'o years," Cathy said.

"Aw, Ma, I knowed lot's about huntin' already."

Cathy smiled and, handed him the bowl of food scraps. "Okay, skedaddle. Git on out thar an' feed the dawg."

Sniffle's doghouse was 15 yards from the back door. As Clay walked out with the scraps, the dog stood up and barked fiercely toward the woods. Clay looked in that direction and saw Speed and Fred standing just inside the wood-line 30 yards away. For a moment, he was scared.

The dogs were watching him, and Fred made a whimpering sound, as if begging for food. Clay told Sniffles to quiet down. He thought the dogs looked friendly, but hungry. He could tell they were hunting dogs and must belong to somebody. His Grandpa had a foxhound, and he was about the same size as Fred. He didn't have the heart to let the dogs go hungry, so he slowly walked toward them and set the bowl on the ground. "Hey boy, are ye hungry?"

Fred walked toward him with his head down and his tail dragging. Clay walked back and stood next to Sniffles. Fred and Speed walked cautiously toward the bowl.

Sniffles whined. Clay whispered, "Don't worry none Sniffles, I'll go in the house an' gitcha some more vittles in a minute." The boy stood quietly and watched the dogs devour the food.

After they ate, Fred looked at Clay with his soft brown eyes to let him know he was grateful for the food. And Speed also looked up as if to say *thank you.* Then they turned and made their way back into the woods.

They continued their journey, yearning for home. The land that lay before them was rough Appalachian Mountains country filled with steep hills and large mountains, all the way to Coalfield.

The dogs had 60 miles to go before reaching home. Their undying devotion to John pushed them forward.

They pushed themselves hard most of the day. By late evening, they were heading southwest, around a large mountain, which took them several miles out of their way. After they got around the mountain, they found the right direction of travel. Three days and two mile southeast of Creekmore, Kentucky on Little Rock Creek Road, they were weary and thirsty, but weren't ready to stop and rest. They were trotting at a steady pace; making their way towards the Tennessee state line.

Several hours later, they walked through tall grass at the edge of a hayfield looking for a place to lie down. Thunder roared in the distance. They knew rain was on the way. The sky had turned dark, and a storm was moving in. They needed to find shelter.

Lighting flashed across the dark sky and rain came down heavily. A crash of thunder boomed as they approached an opened field. The rain was cold and sharp, like needles. They ran, making their way across the field toward a barn, which was situated several yards from a large white farmhouse, with a porch across the front.

Several cows lay in the field to their right. As the dogs approached the barn, they saw an open side door, and they went inside. They heard a horse in the end stall and the sound of a cow bellowing at the other end of the barn. It felt safe, and it was dry. They found soft, warm hay in the corner of the barn, and they lay down listening to the heavy rain falling on the roof. It didn't take long for them to fall asleep.

Just before dawn, a noise outside the barn wakened them. They stood up and started toward the side door. Just steps from the fresh air, the owner of the farm, Jim Ford, swung the door open. The man was in his early forties, with a short beard, and he wore overalls and a blue plaid shirt. He was carrying a milk bucket and was going to milk the cow. Just inside the barn, he turned and shut the door.

That's when Jim noticed Fred and Speed standing close to the outside wall. "Well, well, what do we got heah? And whar did you two come from?" He asked, in a deep voice.

The dogs remained close to the wall, looking at him. Jim didn't move at first. He didn't want to scare them. He could see they were foxhounds, and he would almost bet they were lost and separated from their owner, owners he had no intention of finding. He was thinking to himself, *I'll get em to trust me, an' keep em fer my own huntin' dawgs. These dawgs shore look like some fine foxhounds.*

He enjoyed foxhunting, but his dog Pete was an old foxhound, and his hunting days were over. He just lay around most of the time.

The dogs didn't know if they should come closer. The farmer knelt down and reached his hand toward them in a friendly manner. They stood motionless. He slowly walked toward the stall carrying his bucket, ready to milk Miss Posy. His ten-year-old daughter, Susie, had chosen the name "Miss Posy". "She had grown fond of the cow, and thought of her as a pet.

Jim thought to himself, *I'll milk the cow, an' show 'em I ain't gonna hurt em', then maybe they'll trust me.*

He began milking Miss Posy and whistling. Fred and Speed remained at the far end against the wall, looking at him. Jim finished milking and went to the side door. He turned toward the dogs. "You two look hungry, I'll fetch ya some vittles in a li'l bit." Then he closed the door.

They didn't know how to get out of the barn. The man seemed harmless, but they longed for their master. Within ten minutes, Jim came back to the barn with dog food and a bowl of water. He opened the side door and put the food and water just inside. He shut the door, and they found themselves locked inside the barn again. They remained in the farmer's barn for four days. After that period of time it was Jim's hope that they would trust him. He was looking forward to having fine foxhounds.

On the fourth day of captivity, Jim walked to the barn holding two ropes. He had decided to take the dogs out of the barn and tie them near his house, next to a shed that would provide shelter.

He opened the side door and cautiously walked toward the dogs. Fred and Speed were standing near the back wall. He slowly reached out his hand to see if they would come to him. Fred approached Jim and sniffed his hand. Then Speed moved behind Fred. Jim patted Fred on the head. "It's okay, boy, I won't hurtcha." Fred wagged his tail. His instinct told him he could trust the man. Jim slipped the rope through Fred's collar and tied it in a knot. Speed was standing near Fred, and Jim tied the other rope through his collar. He noticed a name engraved on Speed's collar: *John Winters.* He thought: *I don't know no John Winters. They must be a long way from home. They won't nary find their way home anyhow, an' now they're my dawgs.*

Jim stood up and commanded, in a deep voice, "C'mon boys, I'll tie ya up at the house an' ya'll kin sleep in the shed. That-a-way I kin keep a better eye on ye." He planned to keep them tied up for a few weeks, hoping they would be more adapted to their new home.

Holding the ropes in his hand, he led the dogs outside the barn. As he closed the door behind him, Speed jerked on the rope and it slid from Jim's hand. The dog ran across the open field with the rope dragging behind him. Fred barked at Speed. He wanted to follow.

"Well, damn, I done lost a good huntin' dawg. He's long-gone now an' I bet he won't be a-comin' back." As Jim spoke, Speed disappeared from sight.

~~ Chapter Twelve ~~

Becky and Laura were sitting at the kitchen table doing their homework and talking about boys and school.

"Do ya still like Terry Walker?" Becky asked, as she opened her math book.

"O' course I do. He's cute. But don't tell 'im I said that," Laura said, as she fluttered her eyelids.

"I think he likes you, too."

"I hope he does. I'm gonna ast 'im if he likes me."

"Good. I'm gonna ast Daddy if I can be on the basketball team next year."

"He probably won't letcha, on acounta they got to wear shorts."

"I know, but if I wear long shorts, he might lemme."

"Whatcha doin'?" Ellie asked as she sat down at the kitchen table.

"Doin' our homework," Laura answered. "Go to bed." She smiled at Becky.

"We're a-talkin' 'bout school an' the basketball team," Becky fibbed.

"Ya cain't fool me, I heard ya. Yer a-talkin' 'bout boys an' I'm a-tellin' Mama," Ellie responded.

"How do you know? Ya didn't hear anything," Laura shot back at her.

"Now don't start a-fussin' er Mama will give us all some hickory tea, an' we'll all get a whuppin'.'"

"Okay, sit down an' we can all talk about boys," Laura said. The three girls started to giggle.

"What's so funny? Do ya kids have yer homework done?" Rosie asked, as she walked into the kitchen.

"Yes, Mama, we just laughin' 'bout school." Becky smiled.

"An' they're a-talkin' 'bout boys."

The girls looked at Ellie and frowned.

"Enuff laughin'. I'll make ya think boys. Ya kids gitcher homework done, take yer bath an' get in the bed for school tomorrah."

All the kids were safely in bed for the night, and Rosie got into bed and snuggled up to John. "I love ya," as she lay her hand on his chest.

"I been a-waitin' for ya to come to bed. I don't know what I'd do without you, Rosie. Yer a better wife than I de-serve." He moved his hand down her arm, letting his fingers explore the softness of her skin. He looked at her, and the soft light of love in his eyes made her lose control of her thoughts. He whispered, "I need ya so much," He pulled her gently into his arms.

"I love ya, John," was her tender reply, as she lost herself in his warm embrace.

He placed his face against her cheek and whispered again. "I love ya too, Rosie."

They surrendered to each other and found complete peace in each other's love. Their breathing in perfect rhythm, their bodies moved together as one. And, for several moments, they were the only two people in the world. For several seconds, time stood still. Trying to catch her breath, Rosie let his love flow deep inside her. Holding him tightly against her breast, flushed with pleasure, Rosie smiled. They shared such a tremendous love that night; it seemed their souls actually touched each other.

The night was magical, and the next morning a new day.

~~~~~

It was early afternoon, and Speed was running full-force, a large mountain caught in his sight. He was eager to see John. The only thing on his mind was finding his way home. He was running southwest toward Oneida, which was two miles away.

As he made his way closer, he was at a steady trot and very thirsty. Near Ramsey Road, he slowed his speed at the railroad track. He crossed the track several times, dragging the rope behind him. His feet ached, and he was in need of water. As he crossed the tracks, the rope slid into the split end of a railroad tie. He pulled at the rope, but it got tighter. He whimpered as he struggled to break loose. A northbound train headed toward Oneida was scheduled to arrive within ten minutes.

It was late in the afternoon, and Stanley Adkins had just come home from school. He was a cute frecklefaced, twelve-year-old, with dark auburn hair. He was in his backyard tossing a ball. He wished he had a dog to play with, but his mom wouldn't let him have one because trains passed by just 40 yards from his back yard. He tossed the ball high into the air. As he caught it, he glanced toward the tracks, and he saw the dog struggling to get loose. Stanley knew the train was due at any moment. He ran from his yard and rushed down the railroad tracks.

Speed continued to pulling on the rope, as Stanley stopped nearby, not knowing if the dog would bite. He said, in a calm voice, "Hold still, an' I'll try an' gitcha loosed."

Speed stopped pulling and looked at Stanley with his sad brown eyes. The rope had pulled tightly against his neck. Stanley grasped the end of the rope and pulled with all his strength to slide it from under the split railroad tie. As he struggled to loosen it, he became increasing nervous. There wasn't sufficient time to go for help, and only minutes left to save the dog's life.

He could hear the train coming around a curve 400 yards away. He knew he must get the dog loose, or it would die on the tracks. Stanley was a softhearted boy. He loved animals, and he strongly desired to become a veterinarian.

The massive machine was traveling at a slow speed as it approached.

Speed also heard the train and started pulling on the rope again. The engineer sounded the whistle as the train moved increasingly closer. Stanley knew he must think of something fast. Time was running out.

"Stop pulling on the rope, I'm tryin to gitcha loosed," he said nervously.

Speed looked up at him with fear in his eyes, as if trying to say, *Please don't let me die, I want to go home.*

Stanley understood the desperate plea in his eyes, as he struggled to free the rope from the railroad tie. The train was 80 yards away, when Stanley realized the dog was wearing a collar. His hands were shaking as he grabbed the collar and unbuckled it. Finally free, Speed ran from the tracks. Stanley began running back to his yard just before the train passed by.

He would never forget the dog, and the way he saved his life. He felt warmth in his heart, knowing he had done a good deed for a trapped animal. He said a prayer that night that the dog would find his way home.

Speed headed southeast toward the mountains. He would always remember the brave boy who saved his life.

~~ Chapter Thirteen ~~

John arrived home from work, opened the front door and walked into the sitting room where Rosie was ironing the children's school clothes. She had just finished the last piece of clothing and was headed into the kitchen to set the table for the evening meal.

He followed her and gave her a kiss on the lips. "I'm sorry I been so hateful lately. It's just hard to accept that I lost my dawgs. I reckon I'm just feelin' sorry for myself. I'd give just about anything if I had Fred 'n' Speed back. I was a-hopin' they'd come back to Arthur's house, an' he woulda called Brook's Grocery Store by now."

"Don't let this gitcha down, John. Ya need to count yer blessin's an' try to remember the good times you had with em," she replied, as she placed another plate on the table.

"Honey, I knowed yer right. Someday, I'd like to get another dawg, but I know there won't never be another team like Fred 'n' Speed." He walked over to then water bucket on a table near the back door. He reached for the dipper, took a drink, and smiled at Rosie.

"Don't worry, John, everthin's gonna work out. You'll see. Ya need to get warshed up. An' would ya call the kids in for supper?" John opened the back door and beckoned the kids for supper. A moment later, the children came rushing through the door.

"Ya kids gitcher hands warshed for supper," Rosie commanded.

When the family had gathered and all were enjoying their meal, Rosie noticed a worried expression on John's face, though she knew he was trying to get his mind off the loss of his dogs.

"Well, tomorrah's Saturday, an' I aim to walk down to Annie Galloway's house to help her sew on 'er quilt. Becky, you 'n' Laura watch the twins while I'm gone. And I wantcha to sweep 'n' mop the sittin' room an' kitchen. I'll be home in time to start supper," Rosie said, as she passed the fried potatoes to John.

"Oh, the women are gettin' together to do some quilt sewin, huh?" John remarked.

"Three of the women from church are gonna help, Wanda, Mary Beth an' Minnie."

"All ye women get together an' do more talkin' than sewin'," John teased, with a smile.

"Now, how do you know what we're doin'?"

"If ever two er three women get together, a fella cain't get a word in edgewise," he said with a laugh.

"Okay, just eat, an' quit pickin' on us women. Ya don't be want me to start on men, do ya?" She shot back at him with a scowl.

"Honey, you know I'm just a-funnin'. I like to gitcha goin' ever onest in awhile. I reckon I'm just tryin' to cheer my ownself up."

"Yes, I know, John, but you can find another good huntin' dawg. Laura, it's your turn to warsh dishes; Becky can help bathe the twins an' put 'em to bed for the night."

They had no bathroom or bathtub, and Becky had to heat water on the stove and bathe the twins in a wash pan. When finished with their baths, Becky placed them together in their baby bed, one at either end. By morning, they were always touching.

Later that night, when all the kids were in bed, John sat quietly in his favorite chair, with his Bible in his hands, and tried to relax before going to bed. He couldn't stop thinking about Fred and Speed. He missed them terribly, and he remembered how they sounded when on a fox hunt. He could almost hear them bark and see them race after a fox. His mind went back to the time they were pups: *Each week, I took 'em in the woods durin' their trainin'. It was funny how Speed would always nudge Fred back so he could get all the attention. I could tell they loved each other very much. What a great team they were! For where one was, the other was right there with 'em.* He sighed and slowly rose from the chair to go to bed.

The night was still and the family slept quietly. Becky and Laura slept together. Ellie, Lula, and Neva slept together in another bed in the same room. Just after midnight Rosie heard one of the kids scream. She hurried out of bed, stumbled and almost fell trying to find the door. "I got it, John. Prob'ly a bad dream," she said.

Becky continued to scream at the top of her voice, "A snake bit me! A snake bit me!"

Hearing Becky scream about the snake, Ellie felt something lying across her stomach. She was afraid to move. Still groggy, she thought, *The snake is lyin' on my tummy. I got to grab it real fast.* She moved her hands toward the long, smooth object that was on her stomach, and grabbed Neva's leg, slunging it to the floor. When Neva landed on the floor, she started crying. "Mama! Mama!"

Rosie found the light switch and flipped it on to see what was happening. The noise and excitement awakened the entire family.

"What in the world is a-goin on in thar?" John shouted.

Lula and Ellie began laughing as Neva was desperately trying to get back into bed.

"Stop laughin'. Mama, my side hurts." Neva, cried.

"Okay, lemme look at your side. Your side looks fine, Neva. Lie down, an' you'll stop a-hurtin' in a few minutes. Y'uns quit laughin' at 'er 'n' go to sleep." Rosie got the three girls tucked into bed and glanced at Becky. She had forgotten about Becky having shouted that a snake bit her.

She was sitting on her bed crying, as she held her finger. Rosie walked across the room and sat down on the bed next to Becky to look at her finger, "Becky, be still so's I can see what's wrong," she snapped. "Lanssake, it's just a splinter. You musta hit the wall er part o' the winda frame."

"She scared me half to death when she got to screamin," Laura said.

"I'm sorry, Mama. You knowed I'm scared o' snakes. 'Member, Daddy killed two snakes outside in the backyard last summer?"

"Well, thar ain't no snakes crawlin round in here now, so lie down 'n' go back to sleep." Rosie removed the splinter, turned off the light and made her way back to bed. Eventually all was quiet, and she drifted back to sleep.

~~~~~~

Rosie got up early Saturday morning to prepare breakfast. Afterwards she walked to Annie Galloway's house to help her sew on her quilt. As she was walking up the path toward the house, she saw Minnie standing on the porch knocking on the front door.

Annie opened the front door. "Howdee Minnie. Well yonder comes Rosie, just in time. C'mon in. I got the quilt frame ready. Wanda 'n' Mary Beth are here, and they already got to sewin'.."

The quilt frame was rectangular-shaped and constructed of four round poles. The frame hung from the ceiling, with a rope tied at each corner. The ropes were to lower the frame when working on the quilt, or to raise it to the ceiling when not in use. Two of the poles had holes through the wood placed four inches apart. The other two had one hole at either end, with a nail through the holes to hold the quilt tightly in place.

Clothes, and scraps of fabric that were no longer needed, made up the quilts. Small squares were cut from the material, and were sewn together to make various patterns.

Every month, the women in the community gathered to help each other sew on their quilts. Rosie enjoyed the friendship and conversation, and found the gatherings relaxing.

"I just wanna remind you ladies that next month y'all need to come over to my house 'n' hep me sew on my quilt," Wanda said.

"Well all get together at yer house soon as we can," Minnie said warmly.

"It'll probly be two er three weeks before I can find the time to help with yer quilt," Rosie explained.

"Me, too," Mary Beth added.

After a time Rosie looked at the grandfather clock in Annie's sitting room and realized it was late afternoon. She needed to start walking home.

When she arrived home, she heard loud noises and giggling coming from the kitchen. She walked to the doorway, looked down and found she was standing in soapy water. To her surprise, Becky, Laura and Ellie had soapy water all over the kitchen floor, as they slid back and forth. Rosie stood behind Ellie and watched.

"Watch this Becky," Ellie said, as she ran a couple of steps and slid across the floor to the other end of the kitchen. The other girls had stopped laughing. Ellie looked up and saw her mother standing in the kitchen doorway. Her eyes widened in surprise.

"Uh, Mama, we jes been moppin' the kitchen."

"It looks like it. Now stop foolin' around and get this soapy water mopped up right now. It's a wonder y'uns didn't fall 'n' break yer necks," Rosie said sternly.

"Mama, Becky 'n' Ellie was doin most the slidin," Laura said nervously.

"Y'all was all slidin'. Ya got water all over ya. Get this mess cleaned up, before I do get mad an' whup all three o' ya."

"Yes, Mama, we will," Becky replied.

"Yes, Mama," Laura and Ellie added.

It didn't take long for them to get the kitchen in order. They had the kitchen floor sparkling clean, in time for Rosie to prepare supper.

The weekend passed quickly, Rosie slowly opened her eyes and realized it was Monday, the beginning of another school day. She fixed breakfast and got the kids out the door. Each day after school, all but the youngest had chores to do. Becky and Laura helped with the dishes, sweeping and mopping. Ellie and Lula had to draw enough water in the big tub to hand-wash the twin's diapers and get out most of the stains. To get the diapers whiter, Rosie washed them in her agitator washing machine. During the winter, they hung the diapers upstairs in the loft, so they wouldn't freeze. Having twins meant they had to wash diapers twice a week. The family worked together to keep things in order.

~~ Chapter Fourteen ~~

Speed was walking down Stanley Creek Road heading south toward home. He was four miles east of Oneida. It was the 15th day since he left Kentucky and the ninth day since he escaped from Jim Ford's farm. He was worn out and panting from thirst. His legs ached, and his paws were sore from running.

He came to a steep bluff at a 70-degree angle. Rocks and loose dirt extended all the way to the top. He began climbing over sharp rocks. Dirt and small rocks slid down the embankment, but he kept climbing, slowly losing his strength, and barely making it to the top. His paws were blistered and yellow matter had formed in his eyes. His throat was dry, and he was desperately in need of a cool drink. He thought of the great care and affection that was waiting for him at home. And he longed for a piece of delicious cornbread that Rosie sometimes baked for him and for Fred. He pushed his body with all the strength he could muster. His heart ached to see John.

At the top of the bluff, he started down the trail heading south. As he moved through thick brush, he saw a small black bear 30 yards away standing upright. The bear went down on all fours and growled.

Barking and refusing to back down, Speed hoped the bear would back away. He was desperate. He must go in that direction to cross the mountain. There was no other way down. The bear shook his head and growled again. Speed kept barking fiercely, trying to scare her off. He held his position and continued barking and snarling. Gradually, she backed up and walked into the wooded area.

Speed made it down the mountain and came to a creek. He was two miles south of Fairview, heading toward Lone Mountain. As sunlight displayed sparkling beams on the water, he drank his fill. He had to find a place to sleep. Dead grass at the clearing of the woods looked perfect, and he lay down to rest.

After sleeping four hours, he got up and began walking again. Just off Smoky Creek Road was Molly and Leon Edwards's house. Leon was a tall, thin man with a short beard and rough country appearance. He postponed shaving as long as possible. They had two boys, Matthew, eight years-old; and Billy, six. Molly was a slender woman with long light-brown hair hanging down to her waist. Matthew wanted to be an excellent hunter, like his dad. Billy loved helping his mom in their garden.

They lived in a two-bedroom wood-framed house with a small porch in front and a large porch in back. They had very little money. Leon helped his uncle skidding logs, earning about $20 a month. To supplement, they had learned to live off the land, hunting wild game in the area and growing fruits and vegetables.

Leon's favorite sport was hunting whitetail deer, which were prolific in East Tennessee.

Leon had gone deer hunting the night before, and, with his hunting skills, brought home a 190-pound ten-point buck. He tied a rope to the deer's hind legs and hung him in a tree behind the house to skin and clean him. After his hound dog, Butch, ate all he wanted of the deer parts, he threw the rest into the woods 200 yards from his house, to avoid the smell.

Speed could hear Butch barking as he made his way through the woods. He tried to avoid houses as much as possible, but he could smell the blood from the meat Leon had thrown into the woods. He approached the deer parts as quietly as possible, and began ton gobble. He had almost finished eating when Butch barked and ran in his direction. He looked about the same size as he, and Speed knew he had no strength to fight with another dog. He ran as fast as he could.

When he was safely away from the dog, he slowed his pace. Three miles southeast of Lone Mountain, he was walking in the direction of Rosedale.

Eighteen days had passed since he left Fred at the Ford farm. Nearing Fort Mountain, land of incredibly large mountains and steep cliffs, he was wearing out and in need of water. His paws were extremely sore and bleeding. Every muscle was ached, yet he had to push on. As he made his way down yet another mountain, he could smell water just ahead. When he reached the bottom, he was rewarded with a creek. He had pushed himself hard all day. He was exhausted, and his stomach was empty again. Just ahead was another steep hill. He was light-headed, but wanted to get over the hill.

Trudging forward, trying to reach the top, he stepped on a dead log, which began sliding. He was so weak, he lost his balance. He slided with the log, and fell 20 feet to the bottom, hitting his back on a rock. He was unable to stand. He lay very still, with deep pain in his lower back. He hoped a wild animal wouldn't come upon him. He knew he was defenseless. Though in pain, he was so fatigued, he dozed off. A short time after dark, a noise wakened him. An owl was screeching in a tree not far away. He still couldn't stand. He hoped the pain would subside soon.

Just before dawn, Speed raised his head. The morning light was dim, and he could see only a short distance. The pain had subsided slightly somewhat. He lay his head down and nodded off again.

At sunrise, he heard a noise and raised his head. There was movement in the bushes nearby, and he saw small trees and brush in motion. He continued to lie still, knowing he couldn't defend himself.

The sun was shining brightly enough to break through the treetops. He tried to stand and saw something leap from the bushes. It was a doe. She also noticed him and quickly jumped back, running through the woods. Feeling a bit stronger, though his back still hurt, he limped as a result of raw paws. He knew he must continue his journey or risk never seeing John again.

He was seven miles from home, and beginning to sense familiar territory. He knew he must be close, and as exciting as that felt, he had to continue hobbling at a slow pace. Two miles beyond, with sharp pains in his hip and right hind leg, he had to stop and rest. He knew if he stayed down too long, he might never get up again.

After a couple of hours, he struggled to stand again. His paws were bleeding more profusely. Each step left a bloody paw print. It took all his strength to walk. He was determined not to give up. He knew home was just over the next mountain. He walked across Walls Hollow Road, and was just one mile from home. In severe pain, each step was taken with difficulty.

It had been 29 days since he left Kentucky and separated from John. On his long journey searching for home, he was near death. However, the thought of seeing John kept him going. Slowly moving forward, and struggling to put one paw in front of the other, he was determined to make it home.

When he saw the cornfield, he knew he was almost home. His legs were shaking as he desperately tried to lift his paws to take another bloody step.

~~ Chapter Fifteen ~~

Autumn in East Tennessee is spectacular, from the Cumberland Plateau to the Great Smoky Mountains; the colors of the changing trees are stunning. Deep browns, bright reds, vivid yellows, intense oranges and brilliant golds. The area's characteristic canopy species are white basswood, yellow buckeye, sugar maple, American beech, tulip tree, white ash, white oak and yellow birch. Other common trees adding to the show are red maple, black and sweet birch, shagbark and bitternut hickories. The small trees and shrubs, also changing color, include hop hornbeam, flowing dogwood, witch hazel and spicebush.

It was late evening in mid-October. John was outside fixing the battery on his panel truck. The starter wasn't getting sufficient currents to turn the motor. He was scraping the corroded battery cables when he noticed motion from the corner of his eye. He looked across the cornfield beside his house, and his heart almost stopped beating. He couldn't believe it.

He blinked and wondered if it was his imagination, or if he was hallucinating and his mind was playing tricks on him. For a moment, he wasn't sure that it was his dog. He almost didn't recognize him. He had lost weight. He was skin and bones, certainly not the same dog he had taken to Kentucky on a hunting trip one month before. He shook his head and took a second look.

It was Speed! For a few moments, John was in shock. The dog was struggling through the cornfield. Each painful step was increasingly difficult. His legs were weak, his paws were on fire, sharp pains stung his back and hip, and he was dehydrated and nearly starved.

John's heart beat faster with excitement, as he ran to pick up his dog. Holding him in his arms, he felt so much joy a tear ran down his cheek.

Relieved that he had made it home and was safe in his master's arms, Speed felt secure and sheltered from harm. He knew his suffering and his long strenuous journey were finally at an end. His strength depleted, he became limp.

As John carried Speed in his arms, he prayed aloud, "God, please let 'im be all right. Don't let 'im die." Many thoughts rushed through his mind: *Speed, how didja find yer way home? Where ya been all this time? Is Fred dead? I cain't believe ya found yer way home as far from Kentucky. Oh, dear Lord, what in the world have ya been through tryin' to get home?"*

He ran to the front door and called, "Rosie, c'mere. Hurry, your not gonna believe this!"

The kids were playing a guessing game in the sitting room and heard him call. They wondered what was happening outside, and they rushed to the front door.

Rosie opened the door. "Yes, John, what is it? Didja gitcher truck fixed?" Shocked and surprised, she saw him holding Speed in his arms.

The kids looked out the door and were as shocked as Rosie. John looked both excited and scared.

"Speed! I cain't believe this. How'd he get here? Is Fred with him?" Rosie asked.

"Oh, Daddy, he looks awful," Becky said.

"Yeah, he's just skin 'n' bones," Laura said.

"Is he dead?" Lula asked.

"Is Fred outside?" Shane asked.

John glanced down at Speed with pity, and then looked at Rosie with a sad face. "I don't rightly know, an' no, Fred ain't with him. Looks like he ain't no more'n a hair from bein' dead. He came up the hill an' he was strugglin' through the cornfield by his self. Seems he just about run his self to death. Fred must be dead, er they woulda stayed together," John said in a trembling voice. "Hurry, get an ol' quilt an' I'll keep 'im close to the back door. I got to doctor his paws, an' cuts 'n' scrapes. If he makes it through the first couple of days, then I'm a-hopin' he'll be all right. He's so weak, he still might die."

"Lemme get 'im some food 'n' water," Rosie said.

"Let's not feed 'im too much the first day on acounta he ain't eaten in such a long time. We don't want 'im a-gettin' ill. Give 'im a li'l of that chicken 'n' cornbread we had fer supper." As he lowered him to the quilt, John recognized that his back was hurt, as he made mournful sound as he laid him down. It was then; he discovered the dog's collar was missing.

Speed tried to raise his head to look at John, whined, and lay down on the blanket again. He had no strength to hold his head up. As John examined the dog, he found that his eyes were red and full of matter, the bottom of his paws had bleeding sores, there were scrapes and scratches on his head and face and cuts on his legs.

John walked into the kitchen and opened a cabinet, searching for medication. He found Vaseline and Epsom Salt. He also found a bottle of rubbing alcohol to clean his cuts. He mixed the Vaseline and Epsom Salt together in a bowl and made a salve. He then found an old sheet and tore it into strips. After cleaning the wounds with alcohol and applying salve to the dog's paws, John wrapped each with the pieces from the sheet. The Epsom Salt would help the soreness and any infection. After treating Speed's paws, John attended to his eyes. He remembered a hunter's trick that Brother Ed had taught him. He placed a small amount of salt on his fingertips and flipped it into Speed's eyes.

Rosie brought the dog water in a bowl, but Speed didn't drink it right away. Rest was what he needed. The first two days, Speed didn't get up at all. He lay on the blanket and slept much of the time. After the second day, his paws continued to bleed. John mixed up more Epsom Salt and Vaseline and wrapped Speed's paws again. By the third day, Speed seemed to have more strength, and his appetite was returning. His eyes had cleared up and were bright again. John felt it would take weeks for a complete recovery.

On the fourth day, he continued to doctor Speed's paws with salve and bandaged them again. Speed couldn't stand very long or walk far. His spirits seemed to be returning, along with his strength. And his appetite had returned. The warm glow from his soft brown eyes told John he was happy to be at home. John was definitely happy to have him home. A week later, Speed's paws were still sore and he continued to lie around much of the time, although his strength was slowly improving with each day.

~~~~~~

Later that evening, John was in his chair reading the Bible when he heard a knock at the door. "C'mon in, doors unlocked," he called.

Bill slowly opened the door and entered the sitting room. John motioned for him to sit down, "Good to see ya, Bill. How ya been gettin' along?"

"Gettin' by, John, gettin' by. My ol' car tore up on me last week, an' I had to put a water pump in it. Took me three days to scare up a used one to fit my car. I finely found one down at Harriman Junk Yard."

"I know whatcha mean. It takes alot a fixin' to keep my ol' panel truck a-runnin'." John lay his Bible on the table near his chair, looked at Bill and asked, "Ya been doin' much huntin' this year?"

"Nah. I went a couple times early spring with Lloyd Watson, my cousin. He left last week an' went up near Kentucky to visit his dad. He lives up thar somewhars near to Winfield. I been workin' like a beaver all summer in my dad's sawmill. Ain't had much time to do much o' nothing. We been gettin' lotsa extry work this year. Ain't been much time for huntin'."

"I reckon my accident shore slowed down my huntin'. I wasn't able to go for a long time after losin' my laig. Then, the first time I go on a huntin' trip in Kentucky, I lost my dawgs. I figah it was hard for the dawgs to go huntin' in new territry. It shore was hard drivin' back home without 'em."

"Yup, I heard aboutcha losin' yer dawgs, John. Maybe ya can find two more foxhounds."

"Bill, your not gonna believe this, but one of my dawgs come on home last week. Can you feature? A month after I lost 'im. Speed's layin' out back."

"What? Speed is here?" Bill's eyes widened.

"That ol' dawg found his way home over all 'em hills 'n' mountains. It's just hard to believe. I was outside tryin' to fix my old battry, when looked up an' seen 'im strugglin' to make his way through the cornfield out yonder. When I first seen 'im, he could barely walk. He came back by his self, though. I reckon I'll never know what happen to Fred. I figure he must be dead. Maybe Fred ran his self to death er got hurt an' couldn't make it on home. I don't know. They always stayed together, so Speed musta left Fred after he died an' tried to make it home alone."

Bill looked surprised. "Speed came home all the way from Kentucky over all 'em hills 'n' mountains? That's hard to believe, John. Lemme tell you that had to be over 80 miles away. Lawdy, he coulda traveled way over 100 miles tryin' to find his way home. It's just a miracle. They hain't no tellin' what that poor ol' fella went through tryin' to find his way home."

"I know. I don't figure I'll ever know what happen to 'em in Kentucky when I was separated from 'em. I reckon somebody musta captured 'em and then maybe they broke loosed an' then only Speed made it on home. Anyhow, when he got here, he had sores on his paws, an' they were a-bleedin'. His head 'n' face had scratches an' he had some cuts on his laigs. He also hurt his back an' right hip somehow. I doctored 'im the best I could."

"Shoot, John, ya always been good at doctorin' critters. It won't be no time 'til you 'n' Speed'll be huntin' again," Bill said.

"He's a-gettin' better, but it's still gonna take more time for him to get well. He's done been home now about a week, and he just lies around most the time. His eyes had matter in 'em, but I cleared em up with salt. His paws are still purty sore."

"I'm glad you got one o' yer dawgs back, John"

"You seen Joe lately? He hain't been by to see me in a coon's age."

"I ain't seen him much my ownself. Joe's been havin' a hard time, you know, with his wife Mary bein' sickly an all. He ain't been huntin' much at all this year. I ain't shore, but I heard the doctor ain't a-givin' 'er much longer to live," Bill said.

"I hate to hear that, Bill. The doctors cain't do anythin' for her?" John asked sympathetically.

"I don't think so. Sump'n about 'er heart bein' too big. Doctor said she was borned that way. Well, I reckon I'd best be gettin' along, John," Bill said. He stood up, and shook John's hand. "Good seein' ya, I hope we can go huntin' again soon."

John returned the handshake, "Yup, I hope so, too, Bill. Stop by whenever ya can."

John went out back to check on Speed. "How's he doin', is his paws gettin' well?" Rosie asked, as she opened the back door.

John slowly unwrapped the bandages before replying, "Oh, yeah, they're a-lookin' much better... I'll leave the wrappin's off this time. They stopped bleedin', an' the redness is gone. Yup, he's pert-near back to his ol' self. After he rests a few more days, he'll be good as new."

"Good," Rosie exclaimed. "I come out here to see if you'd bring some taters in for supper." She asked, as she handed him a bucket.

"I'll get the taters an' be in the house in a few minutes." He looked down at Speed, and the dog looked up at him. "Boy, your pert-near well," John said. It's good to have ya back. It shore woulda been nice if Fred coulda made it. I know you'll never be able to tell me what happen to 'im. I suppose he's dead er ya wouldn't a come home by ye-self. You two shore made a good team. Well, I reckon it's just you 'n' me now, ol' boy." John paused and looked at him sorrowfully. "I know ya miss 'im. I miss 'im too."

He gently stroked Speed's head, and went into the yard to get potatoes from the ground.

~~ Chapter Sixteen ~~

In early November, most of the leaves had fallen from the trees. The air was nippy, and, overall, life had returned to normal. Speed had been home for nearly a month and was much like his former self. It was Saturday morning, and John was in the sitting room reading his Bible. Rosie was in the bedroom sewing. Suddenly, John heard a child crying and screaming outside. "Revrun Winters! Hurry, my paw is trapped! Hurry!"

John rushed to the front door. Clifford Jones' eldest daughter, Brenda, was running toward the house, crying and nearly out of breath.

"What's wrong, honey, what happen?" John reached out and gently touched her shoulders.

Tears were streaming down Brenda's face. "Please, Revrun Winters, my paw is trapped under his car. He cain't git out. Maw told me ta run over here an' gitcha ta help." She gasped, trying to catch her breath.

"Shore, honey, climb in my truck, an' we'll go. What happen? Was he under the car tryin' to fix sump'n'?"

"Yeah, the jack slipped, an' the car fell on 'im," she said as her voice quivered. "We got to hurry, Revrun Winters. Ah hope paw is all right."

"Don'tcha worry, it won't take but a minute er two to get to yer house."

Upon arrival at Clifford's house, John saw Daisy standing by Clifford's car crying and Clifford's feet sticking out from the back of his '47 Ford. He stopped the truck behind Clifford's, got out and walked to the back of his truck to get his car jack.

He shouted, "Clifford, are ye all right? Can ya hear me?"

"John, Ah cain't move. The car's right on my chest. It hurts when Ah breathe. Ah reckon Ah mighta broke some ribs."

He could see that Clifford had placed a block of wood under the car in front of the rear tire. Apparently the block had saved his life, or the impact of the car would have crushed him. He placed his jack under the rear bumper.

"Just hold on, Clifford. I'll try to raise the car a li'l at a time."

"Ah hope he ain't hurt bad," Daisy said. "Ah was a sweepin' the front porch, an' Ah seen the car fall on 'im. Ah was so scairt, Ah didn't knowed what ta do. Kin ya git 'im out?" Daisy asked.

"I think so. I'll jack the car up about four er five inches an' pull 'im out."

"Oh, dear Lord, Ah hope he's all right."

John slowly began to jack up the car, brought it up about five inches, bent down, took hold of Clifford's legs and slowly started pulling. "Tell me if ya start ahurtin', an' I'll stop."

"Ah don't care about the pain, John. Jes' keep pullin', an' git me outta heah, before this thang falls on me agin." His breath was more labored than before.

John pulled carefully until he could see Clifford's face. It was clear, from his expression that Clifford was in excruciating pain. He had no idea what the car might have done to him internally.

"Why don't I drive ya to the hospital, Clifford? Ya best let a doctor check to see if ya broke any ribs."

Clifford started to say something, but John interrupted, "Don't say no more, Cliff. Save yer breath. Can ya make it to my truck? It might be best if ya lie in the back on accounta your pain. Besides, ya might be bleedin' on the inside. Daisy, you can ride in back with him. Brenda, would ya go an' tell Rosie that I'm takin' your paw to the hospital?"

"Shore, Revrun Winters, an' thankee fer helpin' my paw."

"After ya tell Rosie, then git right back over here an' watch the young-ins," Daisy commanded.

"Okay, Maw, but you need ta tell Jake ta mind me. Last time ya went to Brooks, he said he don't have ta listen ta me."

"Well, Brenda, if he don't mind ya, lemme know when Ah git back. I'll try ta be back as quick as Ah kin."

On the way to Harriman, John could hear Clifford groan each time he drove over a bump in the road. The drive to the hospital took 30 minutes, and Clifford was in extreme pain when they arrived.

The doctor ordered chest X-rays, and twenty minutes later he walked into Clifford's room to deliver the news. "Well, Mr. Jones, you've broken two ribs and cracked a third one. I didn't see any internal bleeding. If the car had fallen on you a bit harder, it could've stopped your heart. It's amazing that you're still alive."

"He had a block o' wood under the car. That's what saved his life." John said.

"If not for that block, he wouldn't be here right now Mr. Jones, I'd like to keep you in the hospital a couple days for observation."

"Doc, Ah hain't got no money ta stay in the hospital. I'll be jes' fine at home."

"Of course that's up to you, Mr. Jones, but it would be best. If you feel you must go home, I'll get the nurse to wrap your chest. I'll give you some pain medication to take home with you. Take one every four hours as needed," the doctor instructed.

"Thankee Doc," Daisy said. "I'll make shore he takes it easy fer a few weeks an' don't be liftin' nothin'."

John drove the truck home slowly, trying not to jar Clifford. As a result, the drive took longer than usual, and they arrived home just after dark.

"Thankee, John, I'm beholdin' to ya."

"That's what friends 'n' neighbors are for. Do ya need me to help ya get in the house?"

"Nah, John, Uh, Ah reckon Ah kin make it into the house." He paused and smiled at John, "Ye know, Ah got ta git me a better jack."

"Yessir, that sounds like a dandy idee, Clifford." They all laughed.

"Lemme, know if ya need help with anythin'. I'll be seein' ya."

"So long, John."

After arriving home, John quietly opened the front door, as he knew his family was asleep. As he got into bed, Rosie asked, "Is Clifford all right?"

"Yeah, thank the Lord, he's still alive. He broke two ribs 'n' cracked another'n. The doctor told him to take it easy an' not lift anythin' over five pounds. Said it would take six to eight weeks to heal up."

"That's good." She slipped her arm across his chest and hugged him tenderly. "G'night, John."

"Good night, honey. This has been a long day." They drifted off to sleep very soon.

~~~~~

The twins wakened early and were very hungry. Rosie got out of bed and tried to nurse each baby. She found they weren't as satisfied with her milk as they had been. Sometimes after feeding, they would cry, especially Janie. Rosie remembered that early in the week, her neighbor, Annie Galloway, came to see the twins. As they relaxed in the sitting room talking, Annie noticed how fussy the twins were during feeding. "Sometimes babies do better on goat's milk," Annie had suggested.

Rosie heard John turn over in bed. He slowly opened his eyes and saw her sitting in the chair trying to feed the twins. "What's wrong with Janie?" he asked.

"I don't know. I feed 'er, but she keeps crying like she's still hungry. She's been fussy all mornin'. I don't know what to do for her, John. I was a-talkin' to Annie Galloway a few days ago, an' she said when 'er youngest daughter was borne, she had to put 'er on goat's milk."

"I knowed a fella who raises goats. Ronnie Pemberton has raised goats for years. He lives near to Wartburg. I'll go tomorrah 'n' see if I can get a nanny goat from him. We can try it for a while to see if they sleep better."

Goat's milk was found to be the answer, and Rosie kept the twins on goat's milk until they were a year-old.

~~~~~

John was happy that Speed was again the dog he had been before the trip to Kentucky. He looked forward to getting back into the hunting routine. Certainly, he would miss listening to Fred's unusually melodious bark. Three weeks had passed since Speed's return, and he was completely well.

One brisk morning John went out the back door to check on him, and Speed was nowhere around. He whistled for him several times, but got no response. John considered that he might have gone roaming through the woods, and he'd come back home later in the day.

The day moved slowly, and John was concerned. That evening, just before sunset, John went out to check on Speed again, but he was nowhere around. He beckoned loudly for him, but still no response. It wasn't like Speed to leave home and stay away all day. He felt as he did in the woods in Kentucky. Fright gnawing at him. He walked up the back steps, entered the kitchen, opened the door that led up to the loft and called out,

"Shane, ya seen Speed today?"

"No, dad, I ain't seen 'im all day. He was out back yesterdy."

Rosie was baking one of her homemade yellow cakes with egg-white icing. After placing the cake batter into the oven, she looked at John. "I ain't seen 'im since yesterday at supper time."

Becky entered the kitchen and reached for the empty bowl of cake batter. "I wanna lick the bowl, Mama."

"Honey, ya seen Speed today?"

"Last time I seen him was yesterday evenun'." *Whur could he be?* John wondered. The fact that both dogs were gone once, and now one dog was gone twice, was hard to believe.

~~ Chapter Seventeen ~~

Thirteen miles away, Speed headed north, racing like the wind. He was determined to get Fred. He hoped Fred was still waiting at the farm. With his paws healed, he was strong enough to endure his mission to guide Fred home.

He run all afternoon, and had made his way past Smoky Creek Road, not far from Leon Edward's house, where he stopped to eat his helping of deer meat on his long journey home. He didn't want to meet up with Leon's hound dog Butch again. He made sure he was past their house when he stopped to rest. It was late evening, and he was exhausted. He lay on the cold ground deep in the woods and slept.

Continuing northward, he remembered which houses to avoid and the shortest paths over the mountains. He pushed himself hard, with very little to energize him, except the occasional mud hole or stream to drink from, if he was lucky. The hardships he had to endure were worthwhile, if he could find his brother and take him home.

It had been five days since he left his home in Coalfield, and each day brought Speed closer to the Kentucky state line and the farm where he left Fred. He continued on the trail he had traveled on his way home. Running at a steady pace, there were only three more miles before he reached the farm.

~~~~~~

Fred was lying in the back yard near the shed, with a rope tied to his collar. During the three weeks Speed had been gone, Jim Ford's dog, Pete, died of old age. Jim was determined to keep Fred for his hunting dog.

The sun had risen over the mountain and was casting filtered light over the valley. Speed walked slowly toward the farm and stood in a distant field not far from the house, looking for Fred. He saw Fred stand up as Jim and Susie came out of the barn and started toward the house. They walked up the steps and entered through the back door.

Speed remained quiet, watching the house closely. Twenty minutes later, Jim came outside with a shotgun and walked toward Fred. He reached for the rope tied to the dog's collar and began to untie the knot. He was planning to take Fred fox-hunting.

As Jim untied the rope, Speed barked loudly, sending a message. Fred turned his head and immediately knew the bark. He jerked the rope out of Jim's hand and ran toward the wooded area where Speed was waiting. Jim could only stare in amazement as Fred ran across the field to join his brother. He stood frowning and was frustrated as he watched the dogs meet.

They greeted each other happily, with tails wagging and tongues licking. As he watched the dogs, Jim was filled with anger. *Damn ya. You done made me lose another good huntin' dawg,* he thought. He raised his shotgun and aimed it at Speed. The gunshot sound echoed across the field. The shooter missed Speed, as shot struck a tree behind him. Speed jerked and ran into the woods, heading south in the direction of the mountains. This time he wasn't alone.

As the dogs traveled toward the Appalachian Mountains, Speed led the way, as they struggled over the steep and rugged terrain. Three miles east of Huntsville, they had grown weary. Walking side-by-side in a slow trot they came upon a valley where they saw a farmhouse. The 130-acre farm belonged to the Morgans and had been in their family for over one hundred years. The house was a white, two-story structure with black shutters on the sides of each window, and it had a large porch across the front. Four round pillars extended to the second floor. The beautiful house looked welcoming.

Luke and Sarah gave the house to Robert and Elizabeth as a wedding present. They had two other children, William and Susan. Both had families and lived in Oak Ridge, so Robert inherited the farm.

Robert and Elizabeth had two children: Ben, ten years old; and Tammy, seven. They had lived in the house 12 years.

Robert's parent's house was in the backfield near the woods, 80 yards away from Robert and Elizabeth's house. Built in 1865, the home was a remarkably modern and distinguished house for its time, designed to resemble southern plantation houses. Two large oak trees were in the front yard, and Sarah had a large flower garden at the east side of the house filled with roses, bluebells, chrysanthemums, bleeding hearts, daffodils, marigolds, sweet alyssums, zinnias, purple passage and honeysuckle. She kept fresh flowers in each room, and loved for the aroma to fill the house. Luke and Sarah owned 100 head of cattle, eight horses, six hogs, two dogs and a cat. At the south end of the field was a large barn and a chicken house, where he raised chickens and sold them to market. They had a large apple orchard behind the house, and every year at harvest time the apples were taken to a marketing company in Knoxville.

~~~~~

Three months after Robert and Elizabeth's wedding, Luke and Sarah's house burned to the ground. Robert continued to have nightmares from time to time.

It was around midnight; Luke and Sarah were asleep in their upstairs bedroom. Luke awakened and wasn't feeling well. He had difficulty breathing. He quietly got out of bed, trying not to waken Sarah, and he lighted a kerosene lantern. Carrying the lantern in his hand, he slowly walked downstairs to the kitchen. As he entered the kitchen, he experienced a severe pain in his chest. He fell to the floor and dropped the lantern. He had a massive heart attack! Kerosene spread over the kitchen floor, causing the house to erupt in flames. Sarah was still sleeping.

Soon thereafter, Robert awoke and went into the kitchen to get a piece of chicken from the refrigerator. From the kitchen window, he saw flames leaping from every window of his parents' house. The fire had spread throughout the house. He knew it was too late to do anything. He knew his parents were gone, and a cold chill went up his spine. He wanted to run to them, but his legs began to shake and too weak to support him.

Clutching the counter, he stood staring at the house as the flames consumed it. "Elizabeth, wake up! Mother 'n' Daddy's house is on fahr!" he shouted.

Elizabeth ran downstairs to the kitchen. "Is the house on fahr?" she shouted, in a panic.

"Look out the winda." he replied.

She turned her head to look. "Oh, no! Robert, are your folks inside?"

As he spoke, a lump formed in his throat. "I'm afraid so. It's the middle o' the night."

"Maybe they got out," she said.

"They was sleepin', honey. They aint nothin' we can do. The house is all but gone." As he spoke the house collapsed. He felt tortured from an aching, sorrowful, feeling running deep into his soul. He stood embracing his wife, as he watched the flames incinerate the remainder of his childhood home.

Behind the house was a large round water well. The Morgan family dug it when they built the family home 90 years before. They constructed the top of the well with stones. It stood 32 inches from the ground. Two large poles stood on either side holding a large pole across the top, from which a pulley hung. A rope ran through the pulley to hold a bucket.

After his parents' house was destroyed, Robert carried dirt from the field to fill the hole. It was very deep; he didn't fill it to the top. Some of the stones from the top collapsed and fell inside. He cleared away the rest and pushed them down with the dirt. To keep anyone from falling into the well, he covered the top with boards. The remaining depth of the well was 12 feet, with two feet of surface water at the bottom.

~~~~~~

It was early afternoon when Ben and Tammy got home from school. Elizabeth was watching at the front window for them as they got off the school bus. Soon, they ran through the front door carrying their books.

"Take yer school clothes off before ya kids go out in the yard to play," she said in a gentle tone.

"Okay, Mama. We're gonna play ball in the backyard," Ben answered.

Ten minutes later, they were outside playing, throwing a ball back and forth to each other. The children didn't notice Fred and Speed.

The dogs were walking side-by-side across the field. Suddenly, Fred fell through rotten boards that covered the well, landing in the surface water below. Speed looked down into the well and barked. He repeatedly walked around the well barking.

Ben saw Speed circling and barking where their grandparents' house once stood. Ben turned to Tammy. "Go in the house an' tell Mama thar's a dawg over at Peepaw's place."

"Why don't you go in 'n' tell 'er? And quit tellin' me what to do."

He rolled his eyes. "Never ye mind, Tammy, I'll go in an' tell 'er my ownself."

Ben opened the back door and walked into the kitchen. Elizabeth was preparing supper. He reached for a brownie. "Mama, there's a dawg over at Peepaw's place barkin up a storm."

"Oh really? Keep your hands off the brownies. You knowed it's about suppertime." She looked out the window and saw Speed walking around in circles, barking fiercely. "Well, what's he doin'? Your Daddy'll be on home di-reckly, an' he can check on the dawg, an' maybe he can run him off." She didn't think about the old well.

Tammy came into the kitchen. "That ol' dawg's still barkin' over yonder. Ben, are ya gonna come out 'n' play with me er not?"

"Okay, I'll be out in just a minute. Mama, can we go over yonder an' see what's wrong with the dawg?"

"No-sir-ee. That dawg might bitecha. Your Daddy oughta be home in about ten minutes. You two best get warshed up for supper. It'll be ready right after he gets home."

Five minutes later, she heard Robert enter through the front door. "I'm home," he said. "Is supper about ready?"

"Be ready in a few minutes. Get warshed up," she said, as she placed the cornbread muffins on a plate.

Robert walked into the kitchen and kissed Elizabeth on the cheek. "Supper shore smells good, honey."

"Daddy, a dawg's over at Peepaw's place barkin' an' a-walkin around in circles, actin' queer. He's been barkin' for a long time, ever since we come home from school," Ben said, as he tossed the ball and caught it with the other hand.

"And don'tcha start throwin' that ball in this house, young man," Elizabeth ordered.

Robert went to the back door, opened it and looked across the field toward the area where his parents' house once stood. He looked at Elizabeth with concern, "I reckon I'd best get on over yonder an' see what he's barkin' at. Lemme get my shotgun, just in case I need to shoot sump'n."

"Ya ain't got no time right now. Why don'tcha check on it after supper? The dawg can wait, supper's gonna get cold."

"It'll keep. I'll be right back."

"Ben 'n' Tammy, stay here with me."

"But Daddy might need my help," Ben said, looking disappointed.

Robert motioned for Ben to follow him, "C'mon, Ben, Tammy ya best stay here with yer Mama. Yer too little."

Tammy pouted. "I wanna go too. I'm too li'l fer everthin'."

Robert and Ben walked across the field to the area where the dog was. Speed continued to bark, as he looked down into the well. As they moved closer to Speed, Robert remembered, *an ol' water well onest was here.* As they got closer, he noticed that boards were missing, "Some of the boards are missin', an' it looks like sump'n fell into the well," he said to Ben. They heard a dog barking in the well.

After falling into the water, Fred climbed onto rocks.

"Sounds like another dawg down thar," Ben said. "That's why this dawg was barkin' so loud. I hope the dawg in the well is all right."

"Yer right, son. I hope he's all right too. Hightail it on over to Jeff Turner's house 'n' see if Jeff 'n' Bobby'll help me get 'im out. Then go to the house an' get that rope that's hangin' by the back door. That dawg might be hurt bad."

"Shore, daddy, I'll run faster 'n' greased lightnin'," Ben answered. "After ya get the dawg outta the well, can we keep 'im, daddy?"

"No, son, they probly belong to somebody. This'n looks like a foxhound an' so is the other'n, I'm guessin'. We'll be thinkin' about gettin ya a dawg later, if yer Mama says its okay."

Jeff Turner was their neighbor who lived over the next hill. His eldest boy, Bobby, was 17 years old and incredibly strong. Robert knew if he could get them to lower him into the well, he could bring the dog up.

Robert stood patiently and watched Speed walk around the well, as he barks desperately. "It's okay, boy, we'll get him out if we can," he said, trying to calm the dog.

Twenty minutes later, Ben, Jeff and Bobby came running to the well. Ben was carrying the rope his Dad told him to bring. Jeff looked at Robert and frowned, "Ben said a dawg's down in that ol' water well."

"Yup, I hear him barkin'. I hope he's not hurt. Do ye reckon you 'n' Bobby can lower me down? I'll tie this rope around the dawg, then ya both can pull 'im back up," Robert said.

Jeff turned on his flashlight and looked into the well. "Yup, I see him. He's a-standin' on some rocks against the wall. How deep is the well?"

"It oughta be over 12 feet."

"Well, let's give it a try. Tie this rope around yer waist, an' tie the flashlight round yer neck. We'll start lowerin' ya down real slow, an' if ya need us to stop, just holler back up at us," Jeff said.

Robert tied the rope around his waist, and they began to lower him slowly into the well. From below, they could hear Fred's continued barking. "Be quiet, boy," Robert said. "We don't want no walls a-fallin' in on us. Be still 'n' I'll gitcha out."

Jeff called down, "How far down are ya?"

"I should be 'bout ten feet."

"Holler when ya reach the bottom."

"Okay, ain't much further. Keep goin' slow." Robert dropped down two more feet, and was standing on the bottom. He called up to Jeff, "Okay, I'm thar." He was standing in about two feet of cold water. "Now, I understand first-hand, my daddy's sayin', *'Colder than a well digger's behind'.*"

He heard Fred whining in the darkness. He reached for the light that hung around his neck. He saw Fred standing against the wall on rocks, with his paws covered with water. He reached for Fred and tied the rope around him just behind his front legs.

Robert called up to Jeff, "Okay, take him up slow." Fred remained steady. He knew they were trying to help him. Jeff and Bobby raised him, inch by inch, until he came into the light.

"I see 'im, Jeff called to Robert. "He's almost at the top."

"Good. Don't drop 'im. Careful," Robert said.

In a short time, Fred was at the top of the well, and Speed began to bark happily. They untied the rope from around Fred, and he greeted Speed eagerly. They made whining sounds, as though talking to each other.

"Okay, boy, yer free," Jeff said.

"He shore seems happy. I don't reckon he's hurt bad, do you, Paw?" Bobby asked.

"Yer right, son, the dawg appears ta be okay. The fall just banged him up a li'l. He's a-walkin' okay," Jeff said. He called down to Robert, "I'm gonna lower the rope. When ya get it, holler."

"Okay, go ahead." Robert directed the light on the rope as it came closer. He grabbed it and tied it around his waist. "Jeff, pull me up."

Slowly, Jeff and Bobby pulled until they could see the top of Robert's head. "I see ya," Bobby said. "We ain't got much further to go. Hang on, Robert."

When Robert got out, he looked around and found the dogs were gone. While the guys were pulling Robert up from the well, Fred and Speed ran toward the mountains.

"I'll bet they's good huntin' dawgs, whoever they belong too. I sure hope they make it on home," Jeff said.

"I'm plum tuckered out, son," Robert said. "Let's get on home. Yer mama has supper ready. I'll come back tomorrah 'n' cover up this well. Reckon I'll got to fill it with dirt up to the top this time, an' make shore nothin' else falls in. Thanks for yer help, fellas. If they's anything I can do for ya, just lemme know."

"Glad I could help. C'mon Bobby, I shore worked up an appetite. Let's go eat supper. Come by 'n' see us if ever you can, Robert."

"And y'all come by when ya can. Thanks agin for yer help. C'mon Ben, yer mama's a-waitin' for us." He looked toward the mountains. "I wonder whar 'em dawgs are goin'."

~~~~~

By late evening, Fred and Speed were walking beside each other, traveling down another mountain, past Brushy Mountain Prison near the small town of Petros.

Mountains surround the prison and are very steep. They're covered in pine, oak, dogwood, tulip tree, sugar maple, and heavy brush.

Opened in 1896, the maximum-security prison is one of the oldest in Tennessee, with a capacity of 590 inmates. It was built in the area to ensure that if a prison breakout occurred, it would be difficult for an inmate to make his way over the difficult terrain. Escape attempts have been infrequent, and usually unsuccessful. However, Brushy Mountain Prison closed in June of 2009, and the inmates were transferred to a new prison near Wartburg.

The dogs were extremely tired, especially Speed. He had travelled over 150 miles, with little to eat. As they walked down a country road, they saw a barn in a distant field, but decided it would be best to avoid it, considering the fact they became trapped in Jim Ford's barn in Kentucky. Near the road, they saw a creek, and enjoyed a cool drink before bedding down for the night in a secluded area. Quite exhausted, they lay down on dead grass in the woods.

~~ Chapter Eighteen ~~

The Winters family members were in bed for the night, and all was quiet. John and Rosie snuggled close to each other for a quiet conversation. He gently kissed her. "I shore been blessed a-havin' ya for my wife," he whispered.

"John, your all I need; I'll never love anybody else but you," she said softly.

"If I had my life to do over, I wouldn't want anybody else but you. You've given me such great childrun, an' took such good care o' me since my huntin' accident. You're an amazin' woman, Rosie. What would I do without ya?" He lightly touched her cheek.

She moved closer, resting her head on his shoulder. "John, I'm so thankful for the childrun you give me. The most important thing in this life is family.

It's a shame sometimes, the folks we love can hurt us the most. It tore me up so bad when my mother 'n' daddy separated an' got a de-vorce."

"I know, but we got to accept the bad with the good, or otherwise we won't appreciate the good. That's what life's about here on earth, good an' bad. Even though, it hurt a-knowin' they were gettin' a de-vorce, I know you'd want em' to be happy."

"O' course I want 'em to be happy, but it still hurts."

"We're all just human, Rosie, an' I'm shore our young-uns are gonna disappoint us durin' their lifetime, an' at times, we're a-gonna disappoint them. However, that don't stop us none from lovin' 'em. It's the same thing when we disappoint the Lord. He still loves us. God has his ways to get our attention to keep us in line, the same way we got to correct are kids to keep 'em in line." With a warm embrace, he brought her closer into his arms. They remained close for several minutes, holding each other, until they drifted off to sleep.

~~~~~~~

The next morning a brilliant ray of light over the top of the mountain illuminated every shadow and every vibrant color. It was a gorgeous day. Fred and Speed were crossing Highway 62, making their way toward Coalfield. They walked at a steady pace, with the knowledge that just beyond the next hill was Brook's Grocery Store. Three more miles to travel, and they would be at home.

At the same time, a few moments after breakfast, John drove down to Brooks Grocery, for some needed items.

While in the truck, he admired the beautiful morning, but was melancholy about Fred and Speed, as he remembered the great hunting events he had shared with his dogs. He considered finding another foxhound, but it would take quite a while to train another dog. He was in deep thought as he reached his destination and parked his truck.

Inside the store, Mr. Brooks remarked, "Revrun, I knowed whar you can gitcha another foxhound. My neighbor's dawg just had a litter of pups three days ago."

"I was thinkin' 'bout maybe gettin' me another huntin' dawg. I'll give it some thought, Mr. Brooks, an' letcha know," John said as he put his things on the counter. "I shore do miss my dawgs, but I know I'll never see 'em again." He sighed as he picked up the bags and left the store. *If only I didn't take 'em huntin' in Kentucky so far from home, I'd still have my dawgs,* he thought as he got into his truck. He set the groceries into the front seat and started the engine.

As he negotiated a curve, John saw Fred and Speed crossing the road 60 yards ahead. They were headed toward home! His heart leaped with joy, as he shouted, "Whoopee! Would ya lookie thar? It's a miracle. Thank the Good Lord, my dawgs are still alive."

He increased his speed. He was so excited, he was shaking. He felt as though long-lost children had come home. As he drove up the narrow road to his house, his heart beat rapidly.

The dogs arrived home first. They had gone through the woods and the cornfield, to the front door. They were exhausted, and their paws were sore. They had stretched out, and lay panting by the front door when he arrived.

They stood up to greet him as he got out of the truck, jumped against his chest, barking and whining. John noted that their paws were red and blistered, and they had cuts and scrapes on their faces. *With a li'l doctorin', they'll be fine,* he thought.

He laughed as he rubbed their heads. He was as happy as though he had found a pot of gold. They were his treasure. Love filled his heart and his joy overflowed. It was a dream come true.

With tremendous pride, he looked at Speed. "So this here's why ye left. You went to gitcher brother, to bring him on home. Speed, yer an amazin' dawg." He paused a moment and smiled. "Fred, are ya ready to go huntin? Speed, are ya ready to chase a fox?" Neither dog seemed inclined to run anytime soon." John laughed. "Well, maybe in a few weeks. Lets get some food and water into y'all, and take care of yer wounds."

After doctoring his dogs for a week, John found they were recovering rather quickly. They were clearly happy to be together, at home, and with the one person they loved dearly.

After the children were in bed, John opened the Bible and read two chapters in the book of Psalms. He thanked God for giving him peace and for his many blessings, including the return of his dogs. He thought back to the time when Brother Ed gave him the pups. Brother Ed thought they were special. He believed that too.

Suddenly, his dream came back to him. He tried to remember specific details. *There must be a special reason for my dream er maybe a special meanin'. Did I have the dream the same night Brother Ed passed away? Yes, I 'member now, it was the same night.*

Then a thought occurred to him, *Brother Ed musta knowed about his condition. Maybe that was why he was aimin' to find the pups a home before he passed away.*

He remembered another detail about his dream; *My dawgs was a-runnin' real fast. I never seen 'em run so, fast. Speed almost run his self to death searchin' for home.* He was trying to make some sense of his dream and resolve the similarities between it and what happened in life. *Maybe this was indicatin' that the dawgs would travel many miles, and run awful hard, tryin' to find their way home. The dawgs were a-standin' on the cliff such a far piece away from whar I was, an' I despertly wanted 'em back, much like the way I felt when I lost 'em in Kentucky so far away from home, and was a-wantin' despertly to get 'em back. Maybe my dream was a-tellin me I was gonna lose my dawgs, and somehow they'd find their way back to me. Maybe the dream was a warnin' me 'bout the future.*

The more he thought about it, the meaning of his dream fit together. *Yes, the dream did have a special meanin'. Speed was the first to make his way across the crystal path. When he realized Fred didn't foller behind him, he de-cided to walk back across the crystal path and lead Fred over to me. Maybe the dream was atellin' me that Speed would be the first to find his way home from Kentucky, an' then go back after Fred an' lead him back home, similar to the dream. Fred wanted to walk over the crystal path, but sump'n was holdin' 'im back. Maybe the reason Speed come on home first and Fred warnt with 'im the first time was because Fred was trapped somewhars 'n' couldn't escape as Speed did.*

In deeper thought, he was more convinced that his dream had given him a special message, to warn him about losing his dogs and tell him about Brother Ed passing away. He remembered the peacefulness he felt as he watched Brother Ed slowly rise into the light and disappear. *It seemed Brother Ed and the light come together and joined, and that his body was in a diffrunt form other than his human one, cause the soft glow surroundin' his body was like a special power coverin' his body. It could mean that when he disappeared into the light, at that moment Brother Ed had just passed away and crossed over to be with the Blessed Lord.*

An' I 'member the way the light made a pathway so the dawgs could cross over to join me. An' the way Brother Ed was tryin' to help the dawgs walk on the crystal path to get to me without fallin' into the darkness below, is similar to the way a Christian's life is to remain in fellership with the Lord. We must stay on the straight and narrah path. If we stray from the path, we fall into Satan's darkness.

He thought of Matthew 7:14: *Because straight is the gate, and narrow is the way, which leadeth unto life, and few there be that find it.* He thought about the Bible and the teachings of the bottomless bit, with total darkness that God created for Satan and his angels: *It seems to me we got but two choices, to fall into total darkness, or rise upward into the light.*

Jesus is the light that came down from our Heavenly Father to save the world from sins. He though of the words of Jesus in John 8:12: *"I am the light of the world: he that followeth me shall not walk in darkness, but shall have the light of life."*

Brother Ed's in a peaceful place, an' one day, the Lord will appear in the eastern sky to gather his church. Them that are asleep in Christ will rise first, and all them alive on the earth and are saved shall rise to meet the Lord in the air an' be with Him for evermore.

He began to think more deeply about his dream, and he remembered how desperately he wanted to rise up with Brother Ed and join him in the light. *Maybe the reason why I couldn't rise into the light with Brother Ed was it warnt my time yet. I would have to remain here, doin' the Lord's work, preachin' the Word of God, and by the grace of God, and through the power of God, I might lead lost souls into the light.*

Deeper in thought, John wondered, *Maybe the dawgs had someone watchin' over 'em, helpin' 'em find their way home from Kentucky. After all, the dawgs were special to Brother Ed. Could it be? It seems unbelievable, but then, anythin' is possible.* It all comes together.

He was thankful his dogs were at home, and he smiled as he thought of his many blessings. *What a wonderful God we serve! I know I'll never have riches of material things er money in this life, but I got Jesus: An' that makes me the richest man in the world. For in having Jesus, I got it all, because my Heavenly Father owns it all!*

Quietly, he laid his Bible on the table beside him. As he sat thinking about Brother Ed and what a warmhearted and kind soul he was, he had a pleasant thought. *One day I'll see Brother Ed, 'n' all my friends 'n' loved ones again, when the Lord calls all his childrun home.* With those thoughts, he felt calm and peaceful.

"Rest in peace, Brother Ed."

Ann Eva Graves

True facts about the story:

Back in the early fifties, my dad had two foxhounds named Fred and Speed. The dogs were brothers. I do not know how he got the dogs, as I was only three and four years old at that time. He took the dogs on a hunting trip 80 miles from home, to Kentucky. Somehow, the dogs separated from my dad, and although heartbroken, he had to return to Tennessee without them. Regardless of the odds, somehow, they found their way back home.

One month later, Speed came home, but alone. Dad put salve on his feet, which were bleeding and sore. Speed rested for about three weeks, until his his feet healed, and one day he left. Dad had no idea why he left or what happened, but two weeks later Speed brought Fred back home. I can remember my Dad telling the story, and how amazed he was that the dogs found their way home, from so far away. Other hunters in the community were also amazed, and the story spread throughout the area. No one ever determined how the dogs found their way home, nor how Speed found Fred again. The distance they had to travel was over very steep mountains and rough terrain, in the Appalachian Mountains. The mountain terrain is in the states of Kentucky, Tennessee, Virginia, Maryland, West Virginia and North Carolina.

Speed was an incredible dog, which made his way across the Appalachian Mountains three times. The first time, he almost ran himself to death searching for home; the second time he crossed the mountains, he went back to find Fred; and the third time, to bring Fred back home. It is very uncommon for a dog that is lost so far from home to find his way home again.

Crystal Path

The love and loyalty the dogs had for my dad no doubt gave them a strong desire to find their way back home. My dad loved fox hunting with his dogs, and he cared for them very much. Dogs must feel emotions and love similar to the way we do. Just look into their eyes! Of course, it is hard to understand the way a dog thinks, and how they can discern north from east, south and west. They may go by the sun or the direction of the wind. Who really knows?

My dad was a preacher and pastor at Mosey Grove Church in Coalfield. He worked for Morgan County grading roads, and he cleared the roads across a large mountain for the school bus to pick up children through the area. Otherwise, they would have had to walk several miles to ride the bus. Several children living on the mountain could not attend school during the winter months.

My dad bought a nearby house for one thousand dollars, in which my mother had the twins. One of the twins was born with a heart defect (a small hole in the back of her heart). The heart defect was not known until years later.

When my elder sister was fourteen, burned from a fire, and while in the hospital she had to lie on her stomach, in one position, for more than two months. Dad saved a little girl's life after she drank Clorox. Dad was also in a hunting accident in the Catoosa area and lost his right leg eight inches below the knee. Fred and Speed were with him when the hunting accident occurred.

I hope very much that you enjoyed reading my story!...

In memory of a kind loving father,
Rev. Lawrence N. Sumner
1910-1962

DADDY

Daddy was a preacher man that many folks knew.
He gave his life to God and tried to be true,
For God had blessed him with ten kids and a wife.
He loved them so much; he would have given his life,
Just for all of his children to be in heaven someday.
Yes, this was the prayer I know that he prayed.

The Bible was the book that my daddy read.
For preaching the Word, there's a crown on his head.
Oh! I can just see him in his robe as white as snow,
There with the Savior, and I am so anxious to go.
But how he hated to leave his children behind.
As he left, he prayed that the Savior they find.

He said God was calling him, and he couldn't stay,
He told Mama to raise the children right and meet him in
Heaven someday.
Yes, this is what he told Mama, as he drew his last
breath,
Then his body lay still, and his eyes closed in death.
So rest in peace, Daddy, and wait for me,
Then we can be together throughout eternity.

Written by: Ann Eva Graves

1953

1954

My eldest brother was not in the above photographs (1954)

www.ingramcontent.com/pod-product-compliance
Lightning Source LLC
Chambersburg PA
CBHW060037040426
42331CB00032B/992